TRAVEL
TALES

TRAVEL TALES

40 Years • 35 Countries
350,000 Miles by Train

JIM LOOMIS

Haiku Publishing

ISBN: 978-0-578-79094-7

Book Design: AuthorSupport.com
Editing and Proofreading: ProofYourBook.com

Cover photograph: Passengers in the dome above the lounge car on VIA Rail's westbound train #1, *The Canadian*, get their first glimpse of the Canadian Rockies. The next stop, Jasper, is still 90 minutes up ahead.

Printed in the United States of America

Table of Contents

About This Book

Many of these stories originally appeared in shorter versions on my blog, *trainsandtravel.com*. Also included are several full-length travel stories I originally wrote for major publications like the *Columbus Dispatch*, the *Dallas Morning News,* and *International Living* magazine. Others were written specifically for this book.

A number of stories are about some very unique train trips, which is my preferred means of travel. My best estimates are that I have accumulated about 300,000 miles of travel on Amtrak, 35,000 miles on VIA Rail in Canada, and another 40,000 miles on trains in Europe and Asia.

I've also written here about a number of personal experiences. For example, there's a fascinating incident involving Ray Kroc, founder of the McDonald's hamburger empire, and you'll come across a touching moment with Red Skelton, iconic star of radio, TV, and movies.

There are also a few stories about Hawaii's unique brand of politics, including one incident—never before reported—when the Emperor of Japan was unknowingly a part of a local political feud.

These stories were included because I think they're worth telling and have made this a more entertaining book.

Jim Loomis
Ha'iku, Maui

1

Hawaii, Here We Come!

I often wonder about all the extraordinary opportunities that have come my way. Fate? Luck? Coincidence? Yes, all of that. But without question, my life took a huge turn for the better when I met Frank Fasi. And I might never have come to know Frank but for fate, luck, and coincidence.

In the Spring of 1962, I had been married for two years, and my son, also James, was just a year old. I was anxious to re-locate from Hartford, Connecticut, to... well, almost anywhere.

And then, a letter from an old friend arrived—the first and only letter I ever received from him. Dick had gone through the Navy's ROTC program and had just been transferred to Pearl Harbor. His letter was filled—no, it overflowed—with praise for Hawaii: the weather, the people, the natural beauty. With no additional consideration whatsoever, I said, "That sounds wonderful." And we decided to pack up and move almost a quarter of the way around the globe.

A week or so later—and just two days before we left

Connecticut on our 6,000-mile move to Hawaii—I happened to run into my high school football coach, Ralph Erickson, and I told him about our impending move. "A fellow named Frank Fasi played freshman basketball for me at Trinity College," he said, "When you get to Hawaii, call him."

2

Meeting Frank Fasi

By the time we reached Honolulu, it was sobering to realize we were so far from home it had taken three commercial jets more than eleven hours in the air to get us here. But it was real motivation to start the job search. I made the call to Frank Fasi the very next day.

I passed along Ralph Erickson's greeting and told Frank that I was a brand-new arrival and had a wife and 18-month-old son with me. I added that I was going to start looking for a job immediately and it was my hope that I might use him as a reference.

"You can't give me as a reference," he said, "I don't know you!"

As I was trying to think of an appropriate response, Frank said, "So why don't you and your family come up here and have dinner with us tomorrow night?" I accepted, of course.

It was an incredible evening. Frank was handsome and charismatic; his wife, Joyce, sweet and charming and stunningly beautiful; his kids... well, there were quite a few, but all were remarkably well-behaved.

About 10 o'clock the following morning, the phone rang in our little hotel room. It was Frank, calling to give me the names of two local businessmen who—because it was Frank asking—had agreed to meet me. Almost every day for the next 10 days or so, our phone would ring and it would be Frank with one or two more names.

It was an incredibly generous thing to do... but not unusual. Years later, I learned that many of his most loyal supporters had similar personal stories of Frank's kindness and generosity.

Meanwhile, I was hired as Alumni Director for an excellent private boys' school, moving on after a few years to handle public relations for the local art museum.

Then, in the Fall of 1968, Frank was elected Mayor of Honolulu. Eighteen months later, he appointed me as director of the City's Office of Information and Complaint. I spent almost ten years in that job, not only responsible for the dissemination of information about the activities of this dynamic individual and the municipal government he ran, but for responding to questions and complaints submitted by ordinary citizens.

Frank had a thoroughly pragmatic approach to being Honolulu's mayor. He often said, "Good government is good politics." In other words, if the city government ran efficiently, if we responded to the legitimate needs of our citizens quickly and effectively, his re-election campaign should take care of itself.

That made sense to me, and so, with Frank's approval, we changed the way the Office of Information and Complaint had been doing its business. Instead of keeping meticulous records for every complaint or request for service—a system inherited from the previous administration—we ditched most of the paperwork and whenever possible took care of problems by phone.

Most complaints at the city government level are, in fact, minor problems and easily fixed: a pothole in the middle of a busy intersection, a streetlight shining into someone's bedroom at night, a junk car abandoned in front of someone's house.

The word started getting around: Got a problem? Just call Jim Loomis' office in City Hall and they'll take care of it for you. The interesting thing is that the people in the trenches, the unionized civil service city employees—most of them, anyway—also loved working like that. And certainly, the people of Honolulu appreciated the way their city was being run. I know that's true because Frank Fasi was the Mayor of Honolulu for 22 years and to this day is remembered as the best mayor Honolulu ever had.

He was also the person whose friendship I will always cherish and whose influence shaped my life in so many ways, both during and long after my tour in the City Administration.

Just one example: When I left the City government to run the local Triple-A professional baseball team, Frank sent a letter to all his contributors asking them to support the Hawaii Islanders baseball team by purchasing season tickets to our games. That letter from the mayor resulted in some 600 season tickets being sold.

And after I left baseball to partner with Alan Pollock in an advertising agency, our firm handled all the creative work and media placement for several of Frank's subsequent political campaigns. And I have no doubt that our regular clients took note of the fact that their ad agency was close to the city administration.

I often wonder what my life might have been like if I hadn't accidentally run into my old football coach two days before leaving Connecticut for far-off Hawaii.

3

Words of Wisdom... Most Often Ignored

Travel guru, Rick Steves, is one of my idols. I've read most of his books and seen most of his videos, but there is only one specific quote I can recall. And it is so exactly right, so dead on target, and so painfully obvious that it makes me crazy to know that it is so universally ignored by the average traveler. Here's what Rick says:

> *"There are only two kinds of travelers: those who are traveling light, and those who wish they were."*

And, of course, this is the most fundamental of all travel mistakes, and it occurs everywhere. Probably the biggest offenders are visitors here in Hawaii. The *malihini* getting off the plane with several suitcases stuffed with expensive clothes—something for every day, something else for every evening, and several other garments for "just in case." And, as a resident of Hawaii for the past fifty-plus years, I know that their daytime costume is very probably going to be the same almost every day: T-shirt and shorts with rubber slippers.

Will you need to do laundry if you pack light? Maybe, but so what? The hotel will offer a laundry service and, if you don't want to get hammered with their huge mark-up, ask a few questions and find a local coin-operated laundromat where some authentic and interesting conversation could be thrown in for free!

So, when you start packing for your next trip, think of me or think of Rick... but *pack light!*

4

Australia by Rail

I got to the Sydney station almost two hours early, eager to start my trans-continental trip on the *Indian Pacific*. Crews were busy stocking the train and washing all the windows. And, naturally, other train travel enthusiasts got there ahead of me to check out the consist.

With a half hour to go before departure, passengers began to show up and were directed to their respective cars—excuse me, *carriages*—by members of the on-board crew.

It's difficult to get a good photo of the Gold Class sleeping compartments, but it's where I spent three very comfortable days. The sofa back folds down into a very comfortable bed. The upper berth folds down from the wall. In the wall to the right there are two narrow closets and a door leading into a combination washroom with fold-down sink and toilet, both of which empty directly onto the tracks. With both in the up position and a curtain drawn in front of the door leading into the compartment, the little room becomes a very serviceable shower providing plenty of steaming hot water.

Minutes after our 2:55 p.m. departure from Sydney, the well-stocked bar in the lounge car opened and passengers gathered for a welcoming reception... a good chance to meet some of the people we'd be traveling with over the next three days. Champagne generously provided by Great Southern Rail.

Within two hours after leaving Sydney, the *Indian Pacific* began a climb up into and across the Blue Mountains... not nearly as rugged or spectacular as the Rockies, but more like the Blue Ridge Mountains in Virginia—forested and quite tranquil in appearance. Interestingly, the forest consists mostly of gum trees which, collectively, emit the mist that hangs over the valleys here.

There was a bit of grumbling at breakfast on the first morning. Some of the first-time train travelers had trouble sleeping last night and, truthfully, the ride was a bit rocky. According to one of the train crew, there is indeed a rough section of track in the Blue Mountains. As usual, however, I slept quite well.

The *Indian Pacific* reaches the mining town of Broken Hill at 6:40 on the first morning and coffee, tea, and pastries are served prior to arrival. And—God forbid anyone should feel any hunger pangs—there are two full-on breakfast sittings right after the 8:20 departure.

That allows an hour and 40 minutes for a change of drivers in the locomotive and for topping off with fuel and water. There are two drivers in the train's head end, by the way, and they trade off roughly every two hours.

Some passengers elect to take their personal automobiles

along with them. Other cars are being delivered to people at major stops along the way. There are two auto carriers on our train, located immediately behind the locomotive.

The Broken Hill area is rich in minerals with silver, lead, and zinc in serious quantities. Many of the "hills" around the town are, in fact, made from material dug from the various mines. Passengers who take off on foot to see a bit of the town are advised to wear a hat and to use sun block (Aussies lead the world in skin cancer). I begin by wandering up and down the platform where I have the first of several encounters with the Australian flies, lots of them, buzzing aggressively around my head and face. After ten minutes or so, I retreat to the lounge car and another cup of hot coffee. It is, after all, only a bit after 7:00 in the morning!

By noon, the *Indian Pacific* has taken a hard left and is heading due south toward Adelaide. The dry arid landscape gives way to more fertile farmland which produces an abundance of grain and hay.

More and more wind turbines are being erected to generate electricity here. We passed a double flatbed truck carrying one of the turbine blades. It was fully half a city block long.

Our stop in Adelaide will be just over three hours... time to change both operating and on-board crews, restock the dining and lounge cars, and for many of us to take one of the optional tours. There has been a ferocious heat wave here for the past two weeks with temperature well up over 100 degrees every day. Today is mild by comparison, but I elect to spend our time here in an air-conditioned bus while seeing something of the capital city of South Australia.

During the *Indian Pacific's* 3-and-a-half-hour stopover in

Adelaide, I took a bus tour of the city. I really like this town. It has an open and comfortable feel to it, well laid out with wide streets and numerous parks.

Halfway through the tour, we stopped in one of the parks where, we were told, the locals come to soak in the great "view" of their city. Apparently, this little rise is what passes for a hill in these parts.

Once underway again, the train heads north, then angles westward, passing through Port Augusta, leaving the Southern Ocean behind and, just as the sun sets, striking out onto the Nullarbor Plain.

Morning finds us rocking along across this incredible, desolate vastness... blistering hot sand dotted with low gray-green brush extending to the horizon and for many hundreds of miles beyond. You'll have to take my word for it, but we passed a herd of wild camels, probably a quarter of a mile away.

About an hour after breakfast, the train reaches Cook, originally established to service the steam trains that stopped here. With the advent of diesel locomotives, the town's original population of some 35 souls declined and is, at the moment we arrive, two ladies.

While passengers wander around Cook swatting at the flies, the two locomotive drivers handle the refueling and the unloading of supplies for the two inhabitants of the town.

The two ladies are busily selling souvenirs to passengers in their little shop. In response to a question, one informs us that the population of their town will double in three or four days when their husbands return from a fishing trip, 150 or so miles due south at the Southern Ocean.

Thirty minutes after our arrival, the *Indian Pacific* is

underway once again. The Nullarbor landscape changes subtly—from no trees to some trees, from yellow sand to red earth—and there are occasional sightings of wedge-tailed eagles and dingos, the wild dogs of Australia. Life on board settles into an easy low-key routine... with cold beverages in the lounge car. Offhand, I can't think of anywhere else I'd rather be at this particular moment.

This must be one of the great deserts of the world. But its name is misleading. Nullarbor comes from the Latin meaning "no trees," but while that may be an accurate description in some parts of this magnificent wasteland, it's a misnomer in many other areas.

After a 30-minute stop at Cook, the *Indian Pacific* resumes its journey, due west across the vast, desolate center of the Australian continent. That's underscored by the fact that we have just started down the longest stretch of perfectly straight railroad track in the world—almost 300 miles.

Table-top flat, dry as a bone and, wherever you look, not a tree in sight... this is just what I expected from the stories I'd heard of the Nullarbor "no trees" Plain.

But, another 40 minutes farther on, I notice the rocks... some as large as oil drums... scattered to the horizon and beyond. There are no mountains for hundreds of miles. How did they get here? And how long have they been here?

It's close to noon now. And hot. I stepped into the little toilet/shower off my compartment a bit ago and it must have been 100 degrees in there from the hot air that was blasting up from the tracks through the 2-inch drain in the floor. But despite the searing heat outside, there is now vegetation in the desert—gray-green brush related to sage and small gnarled trees.

I'm happily distracted for a half-hour or so by a cold beer and some interesting conversation in the lounge car, but when I return my attention to the Nullarbor, it's changed again, there's red earth now, and sturdy full-sized trees with brilliant green leaves. Yet, for all intents and purposes, it's just as hot and just as dry as ever.

Shortly after 6:00 p.m., the *Indian Pacific* slows to a crawl as we near the site of last week's freight train derailment, caused by a sudden rainstorm and flash flood that undermined the tracks. After sitting on a siding for a few minutes, an eastbound freight trundles past, the first train to cross the temporary tracks that have been laid around the mess.

Now it's our turn, and at a cautious 5 or 6 miles-per-hour, our train skirts what remains of the wreckage. The massive locomotives are still lying on their sides but, working with heavy equipment, crews have salvaged whatever they could, broken the wrecked rail cars into pieces and shoved the whole mess into a huge, contorted pile of debris. Five minutes later, the *Indian Pacific* has resumed normal track speed and is heading directly into the setting sun. We're due into the mining town of Kalgoorlie at just about dusk.

About an hour after passing the derailment site, our train comes to a gentle stop at the station in Kalgoorlie. This has been a mining town since 1893 when gold was discovered. We'll be here for just about two hours—time enough for a bus tour of the town.

In many ways, Kalgoorlie still has the feel of a boom town. Many of the buildings are evocative of a much earlier era—several hotels are reminiscent of Victorian times—and there are even three operating legal brothels. Two of the working girls waved cheerfully as we drove slowly passed one of the establishments, prompting our bus driver to note rather mournfully that there were more than 40 such establishments here in Kalgoorlie's heyday.

The town's major attraction is the Super Pit, where gold is mined using "open cut" techniques. There is an estimated 8-9 years of life left in the pit, which is now nearly 1000 feet deep. Mammoth trucks transport 220 tons of crushed rock and it takes six truckloads to yield a golf-ball-size piece of pure gold.

By 10:30, we've all returned to the *Indian Pacific* for our third and last night aboard and our final stretch run—another 375 miles or so to the west to Perth on the shores of the Indian Ocean.

REFUELING AT COOK

The Indian Pacific's locomotive, fueled and serviced, is about to depart the town of Cook, heading due west into the Nullarbor (literal meaning: "no trees"). This is the "driver's" view, looking down the longest perfectly straight stretch of railroad track anywhere in the world: 297 miles. Incidentally, this train is named for the two great oceans waiting at either end of its route. (Jim Loomis photo)

5

Darwin: From One Extreme to Another

In planning this rail adventure, I had given myself two days in Perth. It was not enough. This was one of those occasions when I would have changed my itinerary—adding two or three full non-travel days—but it just wasn't possible.

Having bisected the continent East to West on the *Indian Pacific*, the next step was to do the same, but this time North to South, from Darwin back to Adelaide, on another great train, the *Ghan*.

The night before my flight from Perth to Darwin, I arranged a wake-up call with the hotel's front desk. I didn't believe the woman who said 30 minutes would be plenty of time to allow for the check-in and security process, so I arrived at the Perth airport nearly two hours before my flight was due to depart.

The lady was right: It took exactly 22 minutes to get my boarding pass, check my one small bag and go through security.

By the way, I have learned that Qantas is an acronym for

Queensland And Northern Territory Air Service, which explains why there is no "U" in Qantas.

For 15 or 20 minutes after taking off from Perth on the way to Darwin, we pass over farmlands that look for all the world like much of the mid-western U.S. Darwin is close to the equator and will be very tropical, but everything in between is Australia's vast central desert—barren red earth, scorched by a blazing sun, and virtually uninhabitable.

Darwin, it turns out, is at the other end of that particular spectrum–overcast today with rain off and on, but still very warm. The Novotel hotel has five floors of guest rooms surrounding an atrium with a central air condition system that manages to keep the staggering humidity at bay... but just barely.

A casual stroll to the park just across the street is enough to break a sweat and following a narrow walkway down through the thick, steaming foliage to the rocky beach has me perspiring profusely.

I had scheduled only part of one day in Darwin—I had sold stories on the two train rides, which was the reason for this trip—but a thundering tropical downpour, continuous for the rest of the day, prevented any sightseeing at all. Instead I relaxed in the Novotel's restaurant/lounge where almost all of the help seemed to be young people from eastern Europe, here to learn English, and the menu featured crocodile prepared in at least a dozen different ways.

BACK ON THE TRAIN.

In a complete opposite from the norm, Darwin's train station is a 30-minute taxi ride out of town, well beyond the airport.

When I get there, the rain is coming down in sheets... so that Great Southern Rail, operators of *The Ghan*, have buses there to take us from the terminal itself directly to our respective railway carriages.

In fact, when the bus stops and opens its door, the steps into my carriage are directly opposite. Step off the bus, step on the platform, step up into carriage "H". Now that's what I call service! Once everyone is on board and settled, the *Ghan* gets underway, rolling past a couple of hardy souls braving the torrents to wave good-bye to a departing relative.

The on-board newsletter announced our 10:00 a.m. departure from Darwin and, by a happy coincidence, that's also when the bar in the *Ghan's* lounge car opened. There's nothing like a champagne reception to brighten up a rainy morning. (By the way, I've noticed that on both trains, the sleeping cars are referred to as "carriages" but, for some reason, it's "the lounge car" and "the dining car.")

After riding through the Nullarbor Plain en route to Perth, it's strange to look out the window and see all of the lush vegetation. And the termite mounds! We pass dozens of them— brown towers of earth-colored material piled three to four feet high. There must be *billions* of the little buggers out there, and they're the reason all the railroad cross ties (known as "sleepers" here) are concrete. Clearly, wood just wouldn't work.

I had been told I would be in this part of Australia during the Wet Season, and I am certainly a believer! The ground is saturated, rivers that will be dry in six months are overflowing their banks, and what will be nothing more than low spots in the terrain come October are lakes today. I haven't seen any crocs but, says one of the crew, "step off the train, walk into the bush 30 or 40 feet, and they'll find you."

Just after lunch, and a bit over 200 miles south of Darwin, the *Ghan* eases to a stop in the town of Katherine, a soggy or dusty (depending on the season) town of some 7,000 people. By now the weather has cleared and I head off down the platform to a van waiting to take us on a two-hour tour of the town. Our driver is a 60ish woman who has lived here for more than three generations.

The first stop is at the town's charming museum, with several rooms of interesting artifacts. One display features newspaper clippings reporting on Japanese air attacks against Darwin in World War Two.

One of the earliest **"Flying Doctor" services** was located here, with pilot/physicians responding to emergency calls from remote ranches and farms hundreds of miles away in the outback.

A pioneer of this service was Dr. Clyde Fenton, whose skills as a physician were matched by his daring as a pilot. In the first several years of his "practice," Fenton racked up some 75 minor accidents, officially referred to as "mishaps." His plane was a 1934 deHaviland *Gypsy Moth* and it is on display in a hanger here. The authorities found Dr. Fenton's ever-increasing total of mishaps a bit embarrassing, but Fenton insisted on taking chances in order to reach his far-flung patients. Eventually, a Solomon-like solution was reached: they stopped counting. Dr. Fenton flew with the RAF during World War 2, and died in 1982.

Katherine School of the Air is unique because the 17 teachers conduct classes for 208 students scattered over

800,000 square kilometers—Australian kids living in remote areas or with parents working in foreign countries throughout Asia. Teachers and students are linked by computers and monitors and satellites.

I remarked to one of the teachers that having the students located at all the varying distances from the actual school must be challenging. "Only with Choir," she said. One more example of how the Australians have coped with their unique circumstances.

Back on board the *Ghan* and rolling south again, there is just time for a few libations to sooth parched throats—touring is a strenuous business—followed by a quick shower in the small lavatory that opens off my compartment.

Meanwhile, we've clearly left the wet, tropical climate of Darwin and are now traveling through an area that boasts some actual hills. It's still green out there, but much dryer and not nearly as lush as the country just a few hours behind us. You've got to pay attention, because the Ghan's Australia is constantly changing.

I do need to offer a few words of praise for the food that is presented to us three times daily. The selections tonight were a zucchini, leek and blue cheese soup and a prime beef filet with caramelized onions and baby carrots. Dessert was a rhubarb and ginger ice cream torte, topped by raspberries in a rosella flower syrup.

The following day we're back in the middle of the trackless hot and dry area that makes up most of the middle of the Australian continent. The first to successfully settle and populate this area could not have done so without the camels and, if you doubt that, I suggest you book a trip on the Ghan and spend some time studying the passing landscapes.

By the way, along with the camels, the Australians brought in young Afghans to wrangle the strange beasts. Knowing the Aussie propensity for nicknames, it was no doubt only a matter of days before the Afghan camel wranglers were called "Ghans" and, obviously, that's the origin of this train's name.

As far as I can tell, terrain is the principle difference between this area and the great Nullarbor Plain to the south. Here there are hills, and those off in the distance could even be mountains. And unlike the Nullarbor, there is, we are told, an actual wet season here, when rains can be prolonged and heavy.

The Ghan reaches Alice Springs shortly after 9:00 a.m. and passengers file off the train and onto an assortment of buses and vans ready to shuttle them into the main part of town or to one of the optional tours being offered. Today, my choice is to be on my own, to wander around "the Capital of the Outback" and just let impressions happen as they will.

There are a lot of "backpackers" riding in Red Class on this train and this is where a lot of them are getting off. That term is pretty much applied to anyone under 30, wearing T-shirts and jeans, and traveling on the cheap, and there is an entire segment of the tourist industry in this country specifically geared to serving these intrepid folks.

Stepping off the shuttle bus in the center of town, I feel right at home because at first blush Alice Springs looks a lot like a small town in any hot part of the U.S. with buildings that are right out of the 60s. Just over there is the local K-Mart. And the air-conditioned indoor mall here has a huge Woolworth's as the anchor store.

There are also a large number of Aborigines here, too... all chatting in one of their own tribal languages, of which there are a great many. One individual, a "stockman" or cowboy, cuts a very impressive figure. He's wearing a western hat, long sleeved shirt with a dark blue bandana at his throat, and slim jeans that are cut just so over his western boots. Others, in fact most of the others, are dressed more shabbily, but are moving about their business through the mall, stopping for an ice cream cone or peering into shop windows.

I'm back aboard the shuttle bus at noon and back at the train station 10 minutes later, relaxing with a cold drink in the Ghan's lounge car and swapping stories with other passengers about our morning excursions. The aborigines are mentioned and one man—mid-50s, shaved head, a blunt spoken Aussie businessman on holiday—says, "Most of us aren't very proud over how the indigenous people have been treated in this country." After a brief silence, the subject is changed.

Underway again. Sometime that afternoon several announcements are made that we are approaching the Finke River, described as one of the oldest rivers on the planet and which we will be crossing on a bridge that is 1500 feet long. And—ta-dah!—here it is. The Finke Fiver is wide, all right, but it's bone dry except for a few spots where water has puddled in low spots. (Britannica describes the Finke as "a major inter-mittent river.")

Once again, I'm struck by the one consistent impression one has when crisscrossing this continent: how hot and dry it is so much of the time.

We left the harsh desert during the wee hours and, at the moment, are passing through broad fields from which wheat has recently been harvested. There's been a terrible heat wave here over the past several weeks, but that appears to be over. The Train Manager reports that the temperature in Adelaide will be warm but comfortable when we arrive just after 1:00 p.m.

The train rolls through a long slow arc around the town of Port Pirie. There's a smelter operating here and the principal feature of the company—in fact, of the whole town—is the smokestack which is 200 meters high. That's 656 feet for the metrically challenged.

The *Ghan* is still traveling through farmland, but moving at an easy pace as we pass residential communities that are coming more frequently. Adelaide is up ahead on the horizon and in less than 30 minutes, the second and last of these two extraordinary rail journeys will be over.

It's a recurring phenomenon with me: a feeling of melancholy during the last hour or so of any long-distance train journey. It's happening again as I finish a last drink in the lounge car, pay my tab, and shake hands with two of my fellow passengers in case we miss each other on the platform. In less than two hours, the *Ghan* will arrive in Adelaide, concluding the 1851-mile journey that bisects Australia north-south.

Tonight I'll be in Adelaide—a city I would love to revisit— and tomorrow I'm off to Sydney and a performance of Mozart's *The Magic Flute* at their magnificent Opera House. What better way to spend my final night in Australia?

6

A Conversation with Charlie O.

I seem to be at that stage of life when we spend an inordinate amount of time recalling all the rash and intemperate things done before getting knocked down a few times, and how they helped to give me a different, broader perspective.

One of those incidents on my personal What-the-Hell-Was-I-Thinking list occurred somewhere around 1960, before I moved to Hawaii.

As a life-long baseball fan, I would have killed for a job in the "front office" of a big league baseball team. I sent letters and resumes to most of the eastern teams and created a small file of the polite form letter rejections that trickled in.

Then one day in the winter of 1961, I happened to spot a small item in *The Sporting News*: Charles O. Finley, owner of the Oakland A's, had just fired his team's traveling secretary.

(The traveling secretary is, in effect, a major league team's tour director, making all necessary travel arrangements for players, coaches, trainers and everyone else in the entourage whenever the ball club is on the road playing in their opponents' home ballparks. It is, I now know, a difficult, thankless job—one for which I was unqualified in almost every conceivable way.)

At the time, however, I picked up the phone and dialed the Oakland A's "General Offices" number, determined to get my name into consideration that very day. What follows is a verbatim account of the ensuing conversation.

Sound:	(Telephone ringing, being answered)
Male voice:	Oakland A's.
Me:	Mr. Finley, please.
Male voice:	This is Finley.
Me (startled):	Oh... uh... well, sir, I'm calling to apply for the traveling secretary job.
Finley:	You have a job now?
Me:	Yes, sir, I'm...
Finley:	What're they paying you?
Me:	$17,000 a year, sir.
Finley:	Stay where you are.
Sound:	(Telephone disconnecting.)

7

The Mayor Got It Done!

Frank Fasi was Mayor of Honolulu for a total of 22 years and, if one had to point to any single event that set him on a course of eventually being acknowledged as the best mayor in the city's history, it was a bus strike.

The bus company serving Oahu for the years after World War 2 was owned by a tough old guy by the name of Harry Weinberg. Harry wanted to get out of the bus business, and he seized on the expiration of his contract with the Teamsters union as his chance.

Weinberg's plan was simple: (1) allow the existing contract with the Teamsters to lapse; (2) refuse to make any serious offers to the union for a new contract, eventually forcing a strike; (3) continue to stall, letting the people of Oahu struggle along without any public transportation; until (4) the city stepped up and actually bought control of the bus company in order to get the buses running again.

Standing in the way of that scheme was Mayor Frank Fasi,

who had already announced that Honolulu should have its own municipal bus system, but without Harry Weinberg.

The mayor had learned that the City of Dallas had been awarded a large federal grant to help in the purchase of a fleet of new buses. With City Attorney Paul Devens, Fasi flew to Texas intending to buy as many of their old buses as possible. However, upon their arrival in Dallas, they discovered the transit workers had just walked off their jobs in an effort to get a new contract covering the new buses.

The Dallas officials were delighted to discover there was a potential buyer for the old buses and in fairly short order, with Mayor Fasi pressing, the terms of the deal were agreed upon. However, the federal Department of Transportation could not release the grant money to Dallas as long as there was an existing unresolved labor dispute. And so two outside parties, the Mayor and City Attorney from Honolulu, whose only interest was in a speedy resolution of the dispute, ended up mediating a settlement between the two parties.

That agreement freed up the federal funds for Dallas to close their deal for new buses and, of course, it enabled Mayor Fasi to complete the purchase of the old Dallas buses and start building a bus fleet for the City of Honolulu.

Meanwhile, back in Honolulu, the bus strike was continuing to make life more difficult for thousands of Oahu residents. To expedite delivery of the buses to Honolulu, the decision was made to drive the entire fleet of 27 buses to the West Coast and load them aboard ships there for the voyage to Honolulu. I've often wondered what all the eastbound drivers must have thought when a caravan of buses passed them heading west, each bus with a large sign showing its destination: "HONOLULU".

The arrival of the first ship carrying some of the Dallas buses in Honolulu Harbor some ten days later set off a media frenzy, including live television coverage by TV cameras sent aloft in traffic watch helicopters. As an entire city watched, a giant crane lifted the first of several buses off the ship's deck, swung it over the side, and set it gently on the huge concrete pier.

And then, always up for the moment, Mayor Frank Fasi climbed into the driver's seat of that first bus, started the engine, and drove figure eights around the stacks of cargo on the pier. The media went crazy, tough longshoremen stopped work and cheered as the mayor's bus drove by. It was a huge media success.

We were also very lucky. Later that day, I learned that the next two buses lifted off the ship had failed to start.

8

I'm Here to See the Mayor

There was always a steady flow of traffic through the mayor's office, most of which was normal City business. But there were also fairly frequent "courtesy calls" scheduled—these meetings were usually quite short and had been granted at the request of a local resident for an almost infinite variety of reasons. Granting a brief two- or three-minute appointment for a courtesy call was a way for the mayor to perform a minor favor for a constituent at no cost to the taxpayers.

Those of us who were in and out of the mayor's office on city business several times a day never knew who we might find waiting in the outer office for one of these courtesy calls.

On one such occasion, I found comedic legend Red Skelton waiting patiently for his courtesy appointment with the mayor. The biggest art gallery in Honolulu was featuring an exhibition of Skelton's oil paintings of circus clowns and it was hoped that one of the City Hall reporters would write something about Skelton and his reason for being in Honolulu.

A small man—at least that's how I remember him—Skelton was sitting patiently by himself waiting for whoever was meeting with the mayor to conclude their business. I walked over, introduced myself, and apologized for the delay. He smiled and dismissed that with a wave, saying he was sure the mayor was a very busy man.

I said I hoped he was enjoying his visit. He shook his head. "I'm sorry, but the truth is, I don't like these promotional tours," he said. "Everyone I meet is disappointed if I'm not funny. No one can be funny all the time. The pressure is awful."

It was really quite sad.

9

The Polar Bears of Hudson Bay

Reprinted with the permission of the Columbus Dispatch

VIA Rail's train #693 trundles out of the Winnipeg station at five minutes past noon, beginning its twice-weekly run to the little town of Churchill, Manitoba, almost 1,100 miles to the north. There will be 25 stops along the way.

Most of us aboard on this late October day are tourists hoping to see the polar bears that come into the Churchill area about this time of year, waiting for Hudson Bay to freeze over. The bears spend each winter out on the ice, many miles from shore, hunting seals, their primary source of food.

Throughout the afternoon, the train rocks along, passing great, broad fields lying fallow after the fall grain harvest. The coaches toward the front of the train are where the locals have settled, many boarding or leaving the train at one of the tiny hamlets along the route. Tourists occupy most of the accommodations in the one sleeping car. So far, I've met an elderly man from New Jersey, two couples from Custer, South Dakota (the men are law partners); a bookish single woman from Australia; and an aristocratic elderly woman from Cologne in Germany. It's a diverse group, but with a common purpose: to see the bears.

VIA Rail dining cars feature communal seating and my companions at dinner are a Swiss man in the shipping business, a young Asian woman who says she's "from Montreal and sometimes Tallahassee", and a gruff, bearded farmer from neighboring Saskatchewan province, who raises what I gather are vast quantities of wheat, canola, and peas. When I return to my compartment, the train attendant has lowered my berth and I'm soon under the down comforter, lights out, watching the shadowy outline of evergreens sliding by outside my window.

Morning reveals a mostly flat terrain with scrubby trees that become shorter and scrubbier the farther north we go— long stretches of tangled wilderness frequently broken up by streams and small lakes, just crusting over with ice and most featuring rounded beaver lodges.

The train frequently slows to a crawl as it passes over stretches of track laid on permafrost which has softened and become spongy. No matter, these and other factors have clearly been taken into account, for our train eases to a stop in Churchill at 7:05 the next morning, just five minutes behind schedule.

There's a heavy overcast and it's quite raw—hardly a surprise, since we're now just 600 miles south of the Arctic Circle—and, right over there behind that row of darkened buildings, is Hudson Bay, its frigid gray water churning against the rocky shore.

Tomorrow I've scheduled a full day out on the tundra in the hope of seeing bears. This morning, however, I'm driving to the Churchill Northern Studies Center some 20 kilometers out of town to meet with Michael Goodyear, its executive director. His facility is home to students and researchers with a common passion: learning more about this vast area and how to preserve it and the wildlife found here.

Goodyear is a 40ish friendly man, clad in the standard unisex uniform for these parts: flannel shirt, jeans and thick-soled boots. He offers me a cup of coffee and, after a few pleasantries, our conversation turns to the many and varied circumstances affecting area wildlife.

The problem in a nutshell, says Goodyear, is global warming. And he is emphatic: the planet is indeed warming and that is a fact beyond dispute. The only possible controversy, he says, is the extent to which the warming is "human driven."

But whatever the cause, he says, warming is having an effect on the polar bears here. Hudson Bay is freezing later and thawing earlier, allowing less time for the bears to fatten up on seals. That, in turn, means bears gain less weight over the winter and they are therefore less prepared for what amounts to their summer-long fast.

Goodyear quotes hard numbers: there are now 934 polar bears in this area—a decline of 22 percent over the past 20 years.

But can't the bears simply move farther north where the bay freezes earlier and thaws later in the Spring? Certainly, he says, but there are already other bears north of here, and any given habitat can only sustain a finite number of animals, whether bears or foxes or seals.

I ask Goodyear what his prediction is for the future of these bears. He shifts uncomfortably in his chair and stares out the window for a moment. "I'm an optimist," he says finally, "so I'll give you my most optimistic prediction. It is this: in 50 years the polar bears will be gone from the western Hudson Bay area."

Ten minutes later, I'm once again in my rental car, rattling over the dirt road on the way back to Churchill. The wind has picked up and there are snow flurries when I pull up in front of the Bluesky Bed & Sled, so named because the owners, Jenafor and Gerald Azure, maintain several teams of sled dogs and take guests on thrilling, if bone-chilling, rides. It's cold today, but there's still not enough snow as the sleds and the dogs will be pulling wheeled carts along the rutty trails.

The next morning it's well below freezing, there are 3-4 inches of snow on the ground, and it's still dark at 7:45 when a bus pulls up to take me and a dozen other tourists to the staging area where we climb aboard our tundra buggy. It's a ponderous over-sized vehicle with huge tires, ideal for what passes for roads out here—really just ruts and bumps alternating with low spots filled with water already turning to gray slush as the temperature continues to fall. Operating our tundra-buggy is a garrulous character named Mac, who keeps up a steady patter for some 20 minutes—interesting information about the tundra and the wildlife here.

By now the visibility has worsened and the snow is at least six inches deep. Abruptly, the buggy jolts to a stop and Mac turns to face us. "Now it would be a good idea if we all remained nice and quiet," he says. And he points out into the grayness.

Sure enough, an inquisitive polar bear is ambling across the rutty road, swaying side-to-side as he approaches, peering at our huge vehicle through the blowing snow. Passengers crowd against the windows and begin snapping pictures. I push open a door and struggle out onto an open platform at the rear of the buggy, right into the teeth of the icy wind. My fingers stiffen and start turning numb. No matter. When I look over the side, the bear is right in front of me and I hurriedly click the shutter.

We come across more bears during the rest of the afternoon, including two young males who entertain us for well over a half hour as they roll and tussle and chase each other in circles. "Just a couple of 800-pound puppies," says Mac. "But step outside, and in five seconds those cute little guys would have you for lunch."

The light begins to fail as we arrive at the staging area and transfer onto the bus for the 20-minute ride back into Churchill. Jouncing along in the darkness, I take out my camera and sneak a look at the photo of my bear. And all I can think about is Michael Goodyear's most optimistic prediction.

THESE YOUNGSTERS
PLAY ROUGH!

Two young polar bears tussle in the gathering gloom of a late October afternoon. This photograph was taken from a tundra buggy about 20 miles from the town of Churchill, which lies just 600 miles below the Arctic Circle on the shores of Hudson Bay. Estimated weight of these two young bears—800 to 1000 pounds. *Each*. (Jim Loomis photo)

10

"That's My Uncle Lee!"

In the summer of 1946, my father rented a house for two weeks in the town of Saybrook on the Connecticut shore. Saybrook is where the Connecticut River empties into the Atlantic Ocean—and the house—I remember quite clearly—was set just a couple of hundred feet back from the beach.

At the same time, just 35 miles up the coast at a Navy base in Westerly, Rhode Island, my Uncle Lee was within a few days of being discharged. He was one of the Navy's best—a fighter pilot, flying the Grumman Hellcat from aircraft carriers at night.

It was a bright sunny day—mid-afternoon, as I recall—and the whole family was on the beach when one of us spotted a lone airplane flying parallel to the beach, but well out to sea. Then the blue-gray plane swung into a graceful arc, gathering speed as it turned inland.

It wasn't until the plane had started a low pass down the length of the beach—its engine a deafening scream—that people began to react: children running in a panic, frightened babies wailing for their mothers, dads gaping at the plane and some shaking their fists as it roared by.

My brother Tom and I—he was seven, I was nine—we were jumping up and down, waving at the plane and gleefully shrieking, *"That's my Uncle Lee! That's my Uncle Lee!"*, quite unaware of my father, who was desperately hissing, *"Shut up! Shut up!"*

Uncle Lee put the Hellcat into a graceful arc, circled around, and made another pass, this time not so low and farther out over the ocean. Then he climbed, waggled his wings, and headed north, back to the Navy base, leaving behind a vivid memory that is, to his day, one of the most treasured moments of my life.

Lee Grace celebrated his 100th birthday in August of 2019. I told this story to the assembled children, cousins, nieces, nephews, and friends, many of whom had not heard it before. As the evening was ending, I waited my turn to wish Uncle Lee a Happy Birthday.

He waved that off impatiently and asked, "Did I make one pass or two?"

"Two," I said.

Uncle Lee grimaced and shook his head, "Well, that was dumb," he said. "When you make a second pass, someone gets the number of your plane."

11

Four Extraordinary Moments

I suppose that, under normal circumstances, there may be one or possibly two events that occur in one's lifetime that cause us to pause at that instant and say to ourselves, "I've got to remember this moment." I can claim four.

November 4, 1958: I was at Boston University pursuing the Radio/TV curriculum. Part of our required course of study was to staff the school's faculty-supervised, student-run radio station, WBUR. (It's now the NPR station in Boston.)

On Election Night in 1958, I was given a portable tape recorder—it weighed about 20 pounds— and sent off to report results from Jack Kennedy's campaign headquarters. He was standing for re-election to the U.S. Senate that year, but it was no secret that he was gearing up to run for president in 1960.

Of course, Kennedy won big that night and, when he finally walked in, Jackie on his arm, the five or six of us from various media outlets crowded around.

That was the moment when I learned you can't describe *charisma*; you can only experience it. I was struck dumb. Never asked a single question. But I knew it was an extraordinary moment I would always remember.

September 28, 1960: Less than two years later, I was in Fenway Park in Boston on a raw, misty afternoon in late September. The Red Sox were playing the Baltimore Orioles and it was Ted Williams' final game in a Red Sox uniform. I think it was in the 8th inning, when the man John Wayne always wanted to be came to bat for the very last time. Moments later, Ted Williams ended an incomparable 21-year career by hitting a line drive home run into the visitors' bullpen in right field. As the crowd stood and cheered, and the greatest hitter in the history of the game circled the bases for the very last time, I said to myself, "I've got to remember this moment."

November 22, 1963: It was a few minutes after 8:00 in the morning in Honolulu. I had just arrived at my office at Iolani School and was sipping from a cup of hot coffee when the school's Business Manager, Bing Fai Lau, appeared at my doorway. He had a stricken look on his face and he said in a hoarse whisper, "Someone shot Kennedy."

I remember staring at him, my mind and my body paralyzed.

"Less than half an hour ago," Bing Fai said. "Looks like he's dead." He looked at me and said, "Get the flag."

He meant the American flag flying at the entrance to the school property. It had to come down to half staff immediately. I jumped up, ran out the door and headed for the main entrance to the school grounds just a few hundred feet from my office. Three Iolani students were already there lowering the flag to half staff. I distinctly remember that all three were

Asian. And all three were weeping. That day—to this day—remains the worst day of my life.

August 7, 2011: I was in Moscow, about to leave the following day on a train across Siberia to Mongolia, then south to Beijing. That night, a dozen of us left our hotel for an informal walking tour of the city. We came up out of the subway, climbed a gentle flight of stone steps, and passed under a simple archway. It took me two or three seconds to realize that I was standing in Red Square! The rest of our small group began to move off across that vast open space towards Lenin's tomb. I couldn't. Not right away. I had to wait long enough to be sure I would always remember that moment.

12

Siberia: In the Middle of Somewhere

It's 2:00 in the afternoon and I'm four days into a 4,000-mile rail journey that began in Moscow and is taking me across Siberia to Mongolia.

The train is a charter with a dozen sleeping cars and three restaurant cars. The equipment is Russian, as is the crew: one male and one female attendant in charge of each sleeping car.

My single compartment is utilitarian and marginally comfortable, while giving the illusion of posh, with deep burgundy the predominant color for the heavy drapes framing the window and the upholstered seat which becomes my bed at night.

At the moment, we're rolling past another small village—a cluster of small wooden houses, their rough unpainted exteriors with—and I find this so very curious—brightly-colored window frames and shutters. Vegetable gardens fill each of the tiny backyards except for worn dirt paths leading to what certainly appear to be privies.

One of our first stops was for an afternoon visit to Ekaterineburg, a major city in Central Russia, modern by almost any standard, but remembered now as the city where the last Russian tsar, Nikolai Romanov, was assassinated in 1918, along with his wife and children.

Another night on the train brought us farther into Siberia and a late-morning stop at Novosibirsk. I think most of us were stunned as we stepped off the train and gaped at the high-rise apartments and the glass and steel office buildings. This is, in fact, the third largest city in all of Russia with about 1.5 million residents who zip around their city on an extensive metro system.

Two more days pass and, as we cross from Europe into Asia, my impression of Siberia has changed: It's nothing like our stereotyped expectations. Of course it's big—vast, really—and the cities we visit are indeed separated by great stretches of forest interrupted by tiny villages whizzing by every hour or so.

But most of these Siberian cities, with their unfamiliar names, are modern metropolises in every way, several with a half-million inhabitants or more. There have transit systems, six-lane boulevards, flashy brand-name hotels, apartment and townhouse complexes, and shopping centers teeming with customers chatting on cell phones or busily texting as they hurry along.

On a free afternoon during our stop in Irkutsk, while finishing a bottle of cola that has never known the inside of a refrigerator, I'm approached by a young man who seems to know instinctively that I'm an American. He's eager to practice his English while I, of course, am interested to learn more about everyday life here in Siberia.

It soon becomes clear that life is not easy for ordinary Siberians like my new friend, Igor. He has a medical degree of some kind, but is currently working in maintenance at a local hospital. From what I can learn given his spotty English, most Siberians are working for wages that would be considered far out of kilter in the west. Top pay for a university professor is about $12,000 a year. School teachers can earn as much as $500 a month, but physicians in private practice make 30 percent less than that. Igor is paid $210 a month at the hospital and works a restaurant job several nights a week to supplement that. Construction workers and unskilled laborers are even farther down the chain.

There are some compensating factors, of course. Most of the apartments, built by the state in the 70s and 80s, have been sold off to individuals at very low cost by the government. And, here in Irkutsk, electricity comes from a huge hydroelectric plant on the Angara River. Igor pays a flat rate of about $10 a month, with no limit on the amount used.

Siberians living in small villages far out in the countryside have quite a different existence. It's all very picturesque from the train, of course, but there are almost no modern conveniences—often not even electricity—and the roads end at the edge of town. The only real link between their very basic existence and the modern world is this trans-continental rail line.

But today, now seven days into my rail journey, the train eases to a stop in Ulan-Ude, capital of the republic of Buryatia and a city of some 400,000 people. It lies in the middle of the Siberian steppes less than 300 miles from the Mongolian border.

As we step off the train and begin strolling through the town, we are all astonished to come across the Theater of Opera and Ballet, at the far corner of the city's central square and recently re-opened after several years of extensive renovation. It is a magnificent facility, and our timing is excellent because there's a performance this evening. Most of us purchase tickets. Cost: US $1.60 each.

That evening, the concert begins when a strikingly handsome man, Mongolian by appearance and natty in a tuxedo, strides to center stage, nods to the orchestra, and launches into a booming *O Sole Mio*. Locals in the audience are comfortably enjoying the experience while members of our tour group seem stunned.

The tenor is followed by a pair of dancers performing a ballet from *Carmen*. The next soloist offers a Puccini aria, then Tchaikovsky is marvelously represented. The evening finally concludes as a beautiful blond woman, stunning in a red sequined gown, performs my personal favorite Andrew Lloyd Webber song: *"Memory"* from Cats. Her performance is the equal of anything ever heard on Broadway.

Another member of our group, a 60ish Dutch woman, is sitting next to me and dabbing at her eyes. "That song was sung at my husband's funeral," she says. "It was quite unexpected here. I mean we're in *Siberia*, for God's sake!"

13

Try Traveling Solo

I'm willing to make a modest bet that people who travel alone enjoy the experience just as much as someone who travels with one or two companions. Perhaps more.

Over more than three decades, my travels have usually involved either a Rail Passengers Association meeting or a meeting of ICOM, the affiliation of independent advertising agencies to which my company belonged. During all those years, it's been my habit to add a week or two of personal travel onto those trips. My wife usually prefers to remain at home here in Hawaii and the net result is that, most of the time, I'm traveling alone.

Prompted by an inquiry from a reader who noticed that, I've given some thought as to how traveling alone is different and the lessons I've learned for making it work.

First—and this is by far the most important thing to remember when traveling alone—*resist the pressure to hurry!* We forget things when we rush and, since we're traveling alone, there's no companion to notice.

Going through airport security is the worst. It's crowded and the guy behind you is always in a hurry to make his flight and he's pressing you. And so you hurry, too, and that's when you leave your laptop or the gift for Aunt Tillie on the belt. You have to keep reminding yourself to slow down because there's no one traveling with you to notice that you left your credit card on the table in that charming little French restaurant.

I've developed the habit of deliberately stopping at very specific moments—immediately after going through airport security or before leaving a restaurant or getting off the train—and taking just 30 seconds to review where I am and what I'm doing. I run through a mental check list: passport, credit card, cell phone, laptop, reading glasses, etc.

Second—pack carefully and pack light: one medium-sized wheeled suitcase and one over-the-shoulder bag. Remember that no one will be traveling with you to help with a heavy piece of luggage.

Remember, too, that the shoulder bag is *never* out of your possession. It's either locked in your hotel room or on your shoulder. In it is your passport, your tickets, your itinerary, a new pen, a small notebook, your laptop or tablet, and—this is very important—all of your prescription medications. *All of them!* Never pack medications in a suitcase that's going to be checked.

In the larger suitcase—the one you *will* be checking—keep a spare copy of your itinerary and a high-quality color photocopy of the page in your passport that has your photo.

Finally, to get the most out of your solo travels, *talk to people!* Start conversations, even if you have to contrive a reason for doing so (a typical ice-breaking line is, "Didn't I see you at Napoleon's Tomb a few days ago?"). Because it's meeting people along the way that makes travel, especially foreign travel, such a rewarding experience.

ALMOST AS FRENCH AS FRANCE

Walk into any of the restaurants or shops in Quebec's Olde Towne and you'll swear you've been magically transported to a picturesque village in Normandy or perhaps it's the Loire Valley. We tend to forget just how very French the eastern part of Canada really is. In fact, Montreal is the second largest French-speaking city in the world! Both sides would benefit from more border crossing points and—better yet!—restoration of a passenger train connecting New York City and Montreal. (Jim Loomis photo)

14

Coast-to-Coast Across Canada

Reprinted with permission from International Living magazine.

In the broad protected harbor of Halifax, Nova Scotia, General Sir William Howe organized the invasion fleet that captured New York City in 1776. During two world wars, convoys of merchant ships loaded with the men and the material of war assembled here before setting out for England across the North Atlantic through the terrible gauntlet of German submarines.

This morning, Halifax is also the jumping-off point for a 6,500 kilometer rail journey taking me from Canada's Atlantic Coast all the way to Vancouver on the shores of the Pacific.

The double glass doors of the Halifax train station swing open and passengers begin moving in small clusters along the platform where VIA Rail's Train #15, the *Ocean*, waits—a dozen cars, in blue and teal livery.

Precisely on time at 12:35 p.m., the train begins to move, and my trans-continental train odyssey has officially begun.

An hour later, we're speeding through wooded countryside, forests of pine and birch interrupted occasionally by small farms. Every few minutes, we cross streams running at the top of their banks, swollen from the Spring thaw. Freshly plowed fields have standing water in low spots.

Around 4:00 in the afternoon, under lowering clouds, we cross into New Brunswick Province and run along the shores of Chicnecto Bay. Farther to the south, it empties into the Bay of Fundy, known for tides that can rise and fall as much as eight feet an hour.

When I appear for my 7:00 reservation in the dining car, the steward seats me with a young woman named Veronica. She's a Montreal native who works for a pharmaceutical company, translating everything from advertising to medical texts from English into French.

Somehow our server instinctively knows to address me in English and Veronica in French, switching languages effortlessly in mid-sentence saying, as she presents me with a menu, "The special tonight is beef stroganoff and (shifting her glance to Veronica) *vraiment, il est tres bon.*"

When I return to my compartment, I find that the car attendant has lowered my bunk, turned down the bedcovers and plumped up my pillows. A dozen pages into a paperback book, my eyelids close.

I waken in the morning to a splash of yellow sunlight on the forward wall of my compartment. We've crossed above the State of Maine during the night and are now heading southwest toward Montreal. I'm about to leave the *Ocean*, however, and catch a connecting train to my next stop: Quebec, capital city of Quebec Province.

We follow the broad St. Lawrence River approaching Quebec through suburbs of tidy little houses with steep-sloped roofs. Up ahead, the city is now clearly visible with the distinctive tower of the Chateau Frontenac dominating the skyline.

This city is thoroughly, proudly, and defiantly French. First settled by French traders in 1608, it will celebrate its 400th anniversary next year. The British captured Quebec in 1759 and it remained under British control until Canada was formed in 1867.

It's the only fortified city in North America thanks to the British who built the massive stone Citadel on a bluff more than 100 meters above the St. Lawrence. The ritualistic changing of the guard takes place here every morning at 10 o'clock—a British tradition presented by French Canadians to mostly American tourists.

Two days later I'm off again, heading west on a three-hour train ride to Montreal, the second-largest French-speaking city in the world. The skies are clear, and the forest trees are leafing out in the warm sun. Halfway to Montreal, we enter dairy country—large farms with herds of black and white Holstein cattle wandering in verdant pastures.

Exactly on time, the train comes to a stop in the Montreal station, which teems with people bustling to and from trains. I'll only be here overnight, so I spend the balance of the day walking around the old town and along the riverbank, with a stop for lunch at Schwartz's Delicatessen, a Montreal institution for 75 years. Their famous beef brisket sandwich is a euphoric experience that must have registered on my face because a young man next to me at the counter nods solemnly and says, "*Extraordinaire, n'est-ce pas?*"

Another day, another train—this one from Montreal to Toronto. The countryside along the way is rural, but the farms are large and prosperous. We pass a picture-postcard horse farm, with a stately main house and several out-buildings. The pastures and paddocks are delineated by pristine white rail fences. Minutes later we flash by an orchard with hundreds of fruit trees—apple or pear—each a giant snowball of white blossoms.

Lake Ontario appears and reappears on our left and seagulls, silhouetted against a mist that shrouds the lake, swoop lazily in and out of the haze.

Toronto's downtown skyline is dominated by towering high-rise office buildings as befits this center of business and banking. With more than 5 million residents, this is Canada's biggest city and the fifth largest in North America. And, as local folk are quick to tell you, Toronto also boasts both a high standard of living and a low crime rate.

The dominant feature here is the freestanding CN Tower, over 550 meters high. On a clear day you can see the far shore of Lake Ontario from an observation deck featuring a glass floor. If you don't have a fear of heights before you step out onto it, you likely will forever after.

The next morning brings clear blue skies and bright sun, a perfect day to begin the last and longest leg of my trans-continental rail journey, a three-night trip to Vancouver aboard VIA Rail's premier train, the *Canadian,* appropriately designated Train #1.

We're not yet in the peak travel season, but this is nevertheless a very long train: three diesel locomotives pulling 21 cars, including coaches, sleepers, two dining cars and four lounge cars, each topped with the classic sightseeing dome.

Well before our 9:00 departure time, a gaggle of passengers has filled the lower level of the bullet-shaped observation car on the rear of the train and every seat in the upper-level dome is taken.

At 9:15, a woman asks, with a touch of petulance, "When are we going to leave?" Her husband shrugs then, pointing forward, says, "Whenever. At least we know it'll be in that direction." Not 30 seconds later, the *Canadian* starts moving, but it's backing up. There's laughter all around, but it's an effective icebreaker. A minute later we come to a stop and, after a brief pause, the *Canadian* begins moving forward, clattering its way through a maze of switches and out onto the main line.

By mid-afternoon, we've entered the vast rocky area above Lake Superior known as the Canadian Shield. This is real wilderness now, a forest of oak, maple, spruce and birch. Fallen trees and saplings bent double from heavy snows have created an impenetrable tangle. Every few minutes we pass a lake, almost every one with a resident loon paddling around on it. There are occasional small frame houses, one with a man filling an inflatable pool in the backyard with a garden hose.

Sharing my table for lunch is a couple from Scotland and we wonder aloud about the people in these little houses. Who are they? What brought them here? How do they make a living? We pass a number of hand-lettered signs for "outfitters," so at least some are catering to visiting campers, hunters, and fishermen.

Back in the observation car, a half dozen people are relaxing with soft drinks. I settle into a seat next to an American couple from North Carolina. He's a chemistry professor and a model railroad enthusiast who happily describes the elaborate layout that has taken over their garage. "It keeps me occupied," he says. "And out of my hair," his wife says emphatically.

Outside, the landscape is more barren now, almost desolate, with trees struggling up out of rocky ground. We are, in fact, in the middle of a large area rich in minerals, the result, scientists say, of a meteor strike millions of years ago.

After a 30-minute stop in Sudbury, the *Canadian* resumes its journey, swinging more to the west and plunging back in the forest. Wilderness or no, a massive infrastructure is required to keep the trains moving. For instance, every switch along this route is connected to a tank of propane gas fueling burners that ignite automatically to prevent the switches from freezing in the winter.

After an excellent meal in the dining car, I collect my toiletry kit and a towel provided by VIA and walk to the head of the car for a delightful hot shower. My bed is made up in the meantime and I drift off to sleep as the *Canadian* passes above Lake Superior.

Evidently, freight traffic delays us during the night because we're behind schedule by almost two hours when we arrive at Sioux Lookout late the next morning. The population here is just 3000, but it's the largest community we've seen since leaving Sudbury, 1200 kilometers behind us.

Throughout the afternoon, the *Canadian* rocks along at a steady 70 mph across Canada's vast breadbasket—endless fields of grain, much of which is shipped back east over these same tracks to Quebec, where it's loaded on ships for Eastern Europe.

The city of Winnipeg comes in the early evening and brings a new complement of car attendants to look after us from here to Vancouver. The dining cars also have new staffs—two cooks, a steward, and three servers in each. Because the train is running late, the Toronto crews handled the first two dinner sittings, then seamlessly turned things over to their replacements for the third. Our new steward says cheerfully, "You got to be flexible to work for a railroad."

My choices for dinner include onion soup followed by pork roast garnished with a glazed onion sauce and a sprig of fresh rosemary. Desert is a delicate apple torte. A very acceptable Canadian *sauvignon blanc* accompanies the meal, the glorious sunset occurring across the vista ahead—orange giving 'way to pink, all streaked with wisps of purple.

VIA Rail's official timetable lists 67 stops for Train # 1, but only eleven are regular ones. The rest are "flag stops" where the train stops only if someone is getting on or off and only on 48 hours' notice. One of these is Brandon North, 140 miles or so west of Winnipeg. There's a station here, but the building is so small it could easily be hauled away on a flatbed truck. The *Canadian* stops just long enough for a young man in a military uniform to board, leaving a middle-aged couple behind on the platform. The woman dabs at her eyes with a paisley handkerchief; the man's expression is grim.

Morning finds the *Canadian* still on the prairie—wheat and horses and cattle and the huge grain elevators, but an occasional oil well has been added to the passing scene.

There's more wildlife today: deer and antelope, bald eagles, wild geese and even sea gulls, congregating in what appears to be a low spot in the prairie filled with rainwater. We trundle onto a trestle crossing a picturesque little valley. A stream winds away to the south with three beaver dams and lodges clearly visible. Every so often we pass small ranch houses, most with trees planted on several sides to help break the prairie winds.

During lunch, someone at the next table is the first to spot the snow-capped peaks of the Canadian Rockies still many miles ahead, but the news prompts an exodus from the dining car as people scurry for a seat in one of the domes.

By 3:00 we've reached the mountains and the *Canadian* begins threading its way through imposing peaks—some with sheer faces of gray rock, others dark green with spruce trees somehow clinging to their flanks. Most of the mountains are topped with snow descending in white streaks toward the valley floor below, then dissolving into icy water that tumbles down into lakes offering mirror images of the peaks above.

Almost everyone in the dome car is snapping pictures through the glass. "I can't get it all in," complains a woman. "It's all too big."

After a 90-minute stop in Jasper for refueling, the train continues its climb into the Rockies, gliding left, then right, then left again as it winds along mountain ridges and cuts through rocky passes, in and out of shadows cast by massive mountains, the snow on their peaks now dazzling white in the late afternoon sun.

In another hour, we meet the Fraser River, swirling around boulders and plunging through crevasses as we follow it to the northwest.

Two black bears come into view on the right side of the train, rooting industriously at the base of a dead tree stump.

As I enter the dining car for my dinner seating, the steward tells us we're passing Mount Robson, at not quite 4,000 meters, the highest peak in the Canadian Rockies. Today the peak is obscured in mist, but many of us dutifully reach for our cameras anyway. Conversation over dinner is about the two black bears—who saw them and who didn't.

The next morning is my last aboard Train #1, and for almost an hour I'm content to stay in bed, comfortably propped up on an elbow and watching the mountain passes gradually give way to a broad fertile valley.

The day is beautiful—bright sun and clear blue skies over a panorama of tidy farms surrounded by lush green fields. Well behind us now, snow-capped mountains provide a magnificent backdrop.

The Fraser River is alongside again, but very wide now and moving at a gentle pace toward Vancouver and the sea. There are several large lumber mills at the river's edge. Thousands of huge logs are simply lashed together upstream and floated down to the mills, emerging as lumber that's stacked, wrapped, loaded onto rail cars and sent back east over these same tracks.

As the train sweeps around a long, graceful curve, the Vancouver skyline appears up ahead. In another hour, we're in the suburbs and, minutes later, the train stops, then begins rolling slowly backwards into the Vancouver station.

A gentle stop and my transcontinental train journey is over. VIA crews are standing by to service the train for its return trip to Toronto this afternoon and, truth be told, if I had the time and if they had the room, I'd be with them. In a heartbeat.

15

Fa'a Samoa: The Samoan Way

I've traveled several times to Pago Pago, the capital city of American Samoa and twice to the nearby independent nation of Samoa, formerly referred to as Western Samoa. The islands that comprise both Samoas are about a five-hour jet flight almost due south of Hawaii. Both offer a seemingly endless number of cultural idiosyncrasies which confound and confuse any visiting *palangi (white foreigner).* The locals just smile and shrug. "*Fa'a Samoa,*" they'll say. It's the Samoan way.

My first trip to Samoa was to make a formal presentation to the Samoan government in which we proposed that our advertising agency be retained to assist them in promoting tourism to their islands. My partner, Alan, and I flew down to Pago Pago, arrived on time at the appointed place to find three men ready to hear what we had to say: the director of the Samoan government's Department of Economic Development, who was clearly the person in charge; the head of the Office of

Tourism; and his assistant, a young man named Pierre, who had attended high school in Honolulu.

Alan and I began our presentation with the three men on the other side of the table listening attentively. We talked about their needs and our capabilities, their target markets, and were about to suggest some different creative approaches when the director raised his hand.

"Would you mind if we took a break," he said, "so the three of us can have a brief discussion?"

Of course, Alan and I agreed. Thinking they would want some privacy, we started to get up and leave the room, but the director held up his hand. "There's no need for you to leave," he said. "We'll speak in Samoan."

And they did, although their discussion didn't last for more that two minutes at the most. When their brief conference ended, the director smiled and said, "You don't have to finish your presentation," he said. "We've decided to accept your proposal."

Alan and I met Pierre, the tourism director's assistant, later that evening for beer and pizza and to discuss getting our new relationship started. Toward the end of the meal, I asked him what had been said during their conference time-out in the middle of our presentation.

The young man smiled. "The director said you seemed like honest people who knew what you were talking about, and he said we should retain your company. It's a good example of *Fa'a Samoa...* the Samoan Way... to make decisions based on an instinctive judgement of another person's character."

16

A Matter of Priorities

Much about dealing with the people in Pago Pago was different. On one occasion, I sent the proof of an ad down to Pago Pago for routine approval, but days went by with no response. Finally, with the magazine's deadline fast approaching, I telephoned to find out if the ad had been approved and was told they had just received it the day before.

Pierre apologized and explained the long delay. It seems that one of the women who worked as a clerk in the governor's office had the responsibility of going to the Post Office every afternoon to collect the day's mail for the Samoan government. However, a favorite niece was getting married on one of the nearby islands and the clerk had volunteered to make the wedding dress. That task, plus the wedding itself, had meant that the woman had missed a full week's work.

Apparently, I remarked to Pierre, it also meant that the

entire Samoan government had received no mail for more than a week, and nobody wondered why.

"Well, you know" said Pierre cheerfully, "*Fa'a Samoa.*"

17

Changing Lanes in Samoa

In 2009, there was a controversy affecting the independent nation of Samoa that sounds more like the plot of a Peter Sellers film.

Traditionally, perhaps because their close-by neighbor was American Samoa, a U.S. territory, automobile traffic throughout Samoa stayed to the right as in the U.S.

But then the prime minister, Tuilaepa Sailele Malielegaoi, issued an edict: at a specific day and time, and henceforth, all automobile traffic in Samoa will switch sides and drive on the *left* side of the road, British style.

Interestingly, there actually was some rationale behind the change: Samoa has a formal relationship with Australia, where they drive on the left, and many Samoans living there ship their used automobiles off to friends and relatives back home in Samoa instead of selling or scrapping them. However, there had been a significant increase in traffic accidents caused by Samoan drivers for whom the steering wheel and gear shift were suddenly on the wrong side in their newly acquired vehicles. The prime minister's order would, it was hoped, correct that problem. and at 6:00 a.m. on the morning of September 8, 2009, everyone changed lanes.

In that instant, people driving American-made cars found themselves driving in "the wrong lane. For reasons unclear, the instincts of a typical driver seem to adapt more easily to the right-to-left shift than a change in the opposite direction.

However, almost immediately, another not-so-small problem became apparent: city buses and jitneys were now discharging their passengers into the middle of the street instead of safely at the curb.

And so, all the buses in Samoa were ordered to be retrofitted: bus doors on the right sealed up; new doors installed on the left. The owners of the buses grumbled and were granted a three-week extension.

Although no amount of logic, tortured or otherwise, has managed to stop the grumbling by opponents of the right-to-left switch, they continue to complain that the change-over caused considerable expense. The P.M. continues to be indignant that his decision was challenged.

18

Welcome to Beijing

Completing the final leg of the 12-day rail journey from Moscow across Siberia to Mongolia, our train arrived on time in Beijing at a grand old train station. It's a busy place with no fewer than 30 trains appearing on the constantly changing departure board, all scheduled to depart at varying times within the next two hours.

The first order of business after checking into our hotel was a visit to Tiananmen Square which, days later in Shanghai, was described to me by a local Chinese as "the political epicenter of China."

First impression of Tiananmen Square? It's huge! At one end is the mausoleum of Mao Zedong (he is always referred to as "Chairman Mao" in China, never simply as "Mao").

There was a great long line of people waiting to enter the mausoleum. I have no idea how many were standing there, but our guide, a personable young man in his early 30s, esti-mated it would be a two-hour wait from this point... and, he emphasized, this was a slow day with smaller-than-normal crowds.

At the beginning of our walking tour, and before arriving at Tiananmen Square, everyone in our group had been given a small radio receiver with an earpiece. Our guide carried a small transmitter and could describe what we were seeing in a normal voice that we could easily hear through this device.

It was in Tiananmen Square, while waiting for a few stragglers in our group to catch up, that I thoughtlessly asked our guide if we happened to be near the actual spot where the young student had stood blocking the tanks during the 1989 protest demonstrations.

A stricken look came over the guide's face. Finally, after staring off into space for several seconds, he said, with lengthy pauses between words, "Well... you see... China is... a very... special... place." There followed a very awkward silence for several seconds, then our guide gave me a very intense look and nodded in the direction of a man standing alone 30-40 feet away from our group. Short and appearing to be in his 50s, the man was wearing a backpack and holding an object the size of a brick up to his ear.

The man stood still, staring into space, as our guide rattled off details about the size of this huge expanse and about the buildings surrounding it. Then the man turned and started walking away.

Our guide—obviously still quite agitated—touched his mouth, then nodded in the direction the man had taken, and then touched his ear. That seemed quite clear to me: our guide was telling me that the man had been electronically eavesdropping in order to hear what our group was being told by our guide.

I can also report that there were literally hundreds of video cameras mounted on metal poles all over the square. Of course, this kind of surveillance around public areas is now common in U.S cities—Times Square in New York City is one example.

Nevertheless, I could not escape the uncomfortable feeling after this incident—that the primary purpose of those cameras was surveillance, not public safety.

Setting all that aside, however, Tiananmen Square is a must-see for anyone visiting Beijing. It is impressive for its size alone, but overlooking the open expanse are the national museum and the massive building where the government meets. Mao's huge mausoleum dominates the far end and, of course, there are the usual heroic monuments honoring the workers. And huge crowds.

I can't explain why I didn't come close to experiencing the same powerful sensation that overwhelmed me when I stepped out onto Red Square in Moscow two weeks earlier. I suppose it was at least in part because our visit to Red Square was at night. But make no mistake: I found Tiananmen Square to be quite intimidating. Because of its size. Because of the surrounding buildings. Because of the heroic statues. And because of the little man with the backpack.

THE LAST FULL MEASURE

This is a cemetery in Bruges, a town in Belgium located in an area where one of the most horrific battles in the history of warfare was conducted off and on from the Fall of 1914 through May of 1915. During that time more than a million men were killed, wounded or reported missing. Every town for miles around has literally dozens of cemeteries like this one. It is a very sobering experience. (Jim Loomis photo)

19

Renting a Car? Be Careful

Avis in Hawaii was a client of my advertising agency, so I have almost always stuck with that company when I have had to rent a car somewhere else in the world.

I'm also a member of Avis Preferred, their loyalty program. It doesn't reward me with free cars or points or miles, but it does tell any Avis employee anywhere in the world that I'm a regular customer and I'd like to think that will help if there are any problems. Besides, I get a discount from Avis because I'm a member of the Rail Passengers Association.

I often mention Christopher Elliott's blog and newspaper columns here, and I can't tell you how many times I've read complaints there from people who have found themselves in disputes with rental car companies. The most common involves billing the customer for alleged damage to the vehicle days after the car has been returned. Often the costs involved are several thousand dollars.

The renter swears that there was no damage to the car when

it was returned, but the rental car company insists there was and threatens legal action.

OK, so in addition to taking photos with your phone of the car when your return it, what should we honest-but-occasional renters do to protect ourselves? Here are a couple of options:

1. The most obvious, and probably the worst choice, is to accept the insurance—the Loss Damage Waiver—offered by the rental car company. Many companies pressure you to buy their "insurance" by speaking ominously about what will happen should you have an accident without it—even an accident that's not your fault. And, as you would surmise, their coverage is expensive. It is, after all, a profit center for them.

2. The next option is to check with whoever sold you the insurance you have on your personal vehicles. Chances are, your personal automobile policy will cover you while you're driving a rental. Just be sure the coverages and limits you have for your personal car will be adequate in the event there's an accident with that shiny new rental car.

3. Finally, and this may also be the answer if you're renting a car outside of this country, contact the company that issues your main credit card. If it's one of the more selective cards and if you've had it for more than a couple of years, covering you for damage to a rental car could be one of the benefits. But find and read the fine print carefully because there can be, and usually are, special provisions. For instance, my credit card company says I must pay for the rental with their card—that makes

sense—and I must decline the coverage the rental car company offers.

Just don't go driving off without protecting your butt in some way, even if it means biting the bullet and buying coverage from the rental car company.

20

Finding a Dream in an Iowa Cornfield

Reprinted with permission from Family Motorcoaching magazine.

Dyersville, Iowa, with a population of just over 4,000 souls, lies in the eastern part of the state some 30 miles from Dubuque and well off the beaten path. Most people would probably consider Dubuque to be pretty far from that beaten path, too.

Dyersville, you see, is where a baseball field was carved out of a cornfield and became the setting for the 1989 film, *Field of Dreams*, in which the ghosts of Shoeless Joe Jackson and his teammates from the 1919 Chicago White Sox come back to play ball again.

The field is still here and, for reasons few are fully able to explain, every year thousands of people from all over the country are drawn to this little Iowa town to see it.

Approaching the Field of Dreams down a dusty dirt road

from the east, my first glimpse is from the far side of a cornfield. But it's not just *any* cornfield. It's the very cornfield into which the ghost players disappeared after their games. Remember? *"I'm melting! I'm melting!"*

Everything is here, exactly as it appears in the movie: the weathered white farmhouse with the wrap-around verandah, the red barns in the background and, of course, the base-ball diamond.

It's late morning on a sunny summer day and there are more than 20 cars in the gravel parking area. Nearby, a dozen or so kids are patiently waiting in line for the chance to step up to the plate and swing at soft pitches being tossed by a man wearing a Red Sox cap.

Out in right field, a father and son are throwing a ball back and forth. After a while, they tuck the baseball gloves under their arms and begin walking in and out of the corn stalks that border the entire outfield.

In the shade of a large tree just off the corner of the farm-house, a family of five has spread a blanket and is in the middle of a picnic lunch.

The Lansing family has owned this farm for a hundred years. Don Lansing, born and raised in Dyersville and the current owner of the property, surveys the activity going on all around him and smiles. "Pretty typical for a summer day," he says.

Lansing has long since become accustomed to having people around his place most of the time, but he still shakes his head when he talks about the knock on his front door during the winter of 1987 that changed his life.

"There was snow on the ground," he says. "It was a lady from

Dubuque. The Iowa Film Office hired her to look for a farm with a two-story house that would be right for a movie."

Dozens of farms in several counties were considered and there were three or four more visits to the Lansing farm over the next few months before it made the final cut. And how did Lansing feel when he got the news? "It was an honor to have my farm chosen," he says simply.

Once the final decision had been made, things happened fast. The baseball diamond was finished within a matter of days. A crew of carpenters descended on the 100-year-old farmhouse and began remodeling the interior, all under Don Lansing's watchful eye. A new stairway to the second floor was installed and several walls on the first floor were knocked out to give cameras more room to follow Kevin Costner and other cast members as they moved from kitchen to living room and back.

Outside there was another problem, one that couldn't be fixed with a hammer and nails. There was very little rain during that spring and summer in 1988, and by late-May the film's producers were starting to worry.

"They came to me saying the corn wasn't tall enough," Lansing says. "I told them, 'Well, it's the drought.' So we dammed up the stream over there and pumped water on the corn around the outfield until it was tall enough so the actors could go in and out." He stares out at the cornfield, remembering. "That was a real dry summer." Then he brightens. "But we've had rain every year since."

The filming was completed on the 15th of August. Almost 18 years later to the day, as we sit and chat on the same porch swing seen in the movie, a man and woman hesitantly approach the white picket fence that separates the house from the baseball field. The man calls out. "Are you Mr. Lansing?"

Lansing gets up off the swing and walks to the edge of the porch. "Yes, I am."

"I'd just like to thank you for keeping all this going," the man says. Then he adds, almost sheepishly, "This is my sixth visit here."

Lansing nods, clearly not surprised. "What keeps you coming back?"

The man pauses, glances at his wife, then shakes his head. "I really don't know," he says.

They politely ask for and get permission to take Don Lansing's photo, thank him again and head back to the field where their son is shagging fly balls in the outfield.

Lansing maintains the diamond himself and pays for the cost of its upkeep with proceeds from the sale of caps, T-shirts and other Field of Dreams items at a busy souvenir stand.

The community of Dyersville has also benefited from all the activity generated by the ball field on Don Lansing's farm. Two new motels have sprung up in recent years and the ripple effect has been a boon for the local restaurants, gas stations and other retailers.

Once again our conversation is interrupted, this time by two couples who approach the fence and politely ask to have their photos taken with the farm house in the background. Lansing says that would be fine and ends up taking the pictures for them. One of the two men asks Lansing for an autograph, then fumbles awkwardly through his wife's purse for a pen and any scrap of paper. Lansing scribbles his name, and the man thanks him profusely.

"No problem," says Lansing. "Thanks for coming by."

"It was an honor," the man said, and all four back away down the grassy slope, almost like courtiers withdrawing from a monarch's presence.

A tour bus comes slowly down the driveway, stops and two-dozen people begin climbing out. There are a lot more people here now than there were an hour ago.

Because there is no admission charged at the Field of Dreams, no one can say for sure how many visitors come here every year. But from the number of names in the guest book he has placed on a stand behind the backstop, Lansing estimates that 60,000 people visited last year alone. What's more, he says, the number of visitors is actually increasing every year.

The people in the tour group drift over to watch the activity on the baseball field where a whole new line-up of youngsters is now waiting to bat. Kids and adults both are scattered around the diamond fielding balls and tossing them back into the infield. There's no yelling, no horseplay. And, as Don Lansing points out, there's not a speck of trash anywhere in sight.

"If all this was a problem, I'd give it up in a New York minute," he says. "But everyone respects the place. They just figure it's their own little piece of heaven."

Is this heaven?

Well, no, it's Iowa... but that 10-year-old about to step up to the plate would almost certainly disagree.

21

Don't Mess with the Conductor!

Over more than 30 years, I've racked up a lot of miles on Amtrak, and I can think of just four incidents where I personally witnessed a passenger causing trouble. That's not to say there aren't people on board many trains that are potential problems. It's just that Amtrak conductors are very, very good at nipping trouble in the bud.

I was reminded of all this when I came across a news story yesterday about some bozo who apparently assaulted an Amtrak conductor on the *Empire Builder*. Big mistake!

I'd guess that booze was involved in this case. Liquor and cigarettes are the two most common problems… people bringing their own booze on board or sneaking smokes in the lavatories or in the vestibules between cars.

When those incidents occur, the conductors deal with the issue very directly: they look the perpetrators right in the eye and say, "Once more, and our very next stop will be yours."

That is usually sufficient, but if the passenger continues to be a problem, the conductor will instruct the engineer to get on the radio and ask the dispatcher to contact the state or local police. A couple of officers are sent to meet the train either at the next station or someplace where the tracks cross a highway.

A veteran conductor told me that once they make that decision, the passenger is never told he's going to be removed from the train. That's just asking for trouble. Instead, the train makes what appears to be a routine stop, as if to let a freight pass, and suddenly the troublemaker looks up to see two big state police officers, handcuffs at the ready. It all happens quickly, almost always quietly and unbeknownst to the other passengers.

The moral of the story is: He who provokes an Amtrak conductor will soon discover there's lots of time for self-reflection at 4:00 a.m. on the deserted platform of the railroad station at where-the-hell-are-we-anyway?

JUST A MAN AND HIS HORSE

Any train trip through the Great American West will be a rewarding experience, especially when it includes the Grand Canyon. If you're a photographer, everywhere you turn there's a great shot. But there's also an element of luck involved. Literally five seconds after I snapped his picture, the rider turned his horse and disappeared. (Jim Loomis photo)

22

A Ride in the Head End

B ack in the mid-90s, I was working on a book about train travel and had spent time interviewing Amtrak on board crews during my many cross-country train trips—conductors, train attendants and dining car staffs.

The one member of the operating crew I hadn't been able to learn much about was the engineer. I had submitted a request to ride in an Amtrak locomotive, but that had always been a rare privilege and I had little hope it would ever actually happen. Imagine my delight when I was notified that arrangements had been made for me to ride in the "head end" of Amtrak's daily *Empire Builder* during a Chicago-to-Seattle trip I had scheduled months earlier.

My instructions were to step off the train when we reached Milwaukee and walk up to the locomotive where an Amtrak employee would be expecting me.

We left Chicago on time and rolled into Milwaukee just before 4:00 p.m., right on schedule. As I left my sleeper, I told the car attendant that I would be riding in the head end for a while. "Wow," he said, "they *never* let people go up there!"

When I reached the lead locomotive (there were two pulling the *Builder*), I found Craig Willett, an Amtrak road foreman, who was to be my escort and guide. He gestured to the metal ladder running up the side of the locomotive and said, "OK, let's go." I shoved my note pad into a back pocket, clambered up the metal rungs and stepped into the cab. The engineer, Bob Kolkman, swiveled around in his chair, grinned, and said, "This must be the writer." Then he eased the throttle forward, the noise level increased to a near-deafening roar, and we started moving.

I was standing in the cab of an F-40 diesel-electric locomotive, since replaced with newer, more powerful engines. Nevertheless, the F-40 was a brutish workhorse capable of producing 3,000 horsepower, but with few of the creature comforts. Air conditioning in the F-40 cab, for example, was accomplished by opening the windows.

To make room for me, the assistant engineer had already gone back to ride in the second locomotive and I was directed into his vacated chair... on the left side of the cab. Railroad engineers traditionally sit on the right side because most signs and signals are on that side of the track.

Forty-five minutes after leaving Milwaukee, we pulled into the town of Columbus, and there on the platform stood a father with two little boys, all waving *at me*, the guy in the left-hand seat. Kolkman noticed and laughed. "They think you're driving," he said. "Better wave back." I did and, before or since, have never felt so puffed up and like such an awful fraud at the same time.

Another hour passed, and I found myself settling into the routine and reveling in the wonderful view from the locomotive cab. The atmosphere was relaxed and friendly, and I no longer felt I was intruding. Willett steered the conversation and answered my questions. Kolkman joined in with an occasional comment, but he was clearly focused on his job. I also noticed that Willett always managed to be facing forward with his eyes on the track ahead even when chatting with me.

As a safety feature, there's a device called an alerter in every locomotive cab. If the engineer fails to adjust the speed or touch the brakes or blow the whistle for a period of 20-25 seconds, a strobe light flashes and a horn sounds. Then, if the engineer doesn't press a button on the instrument panel within a few seconds, the train will automatically come to a stop.

Kolkman was constantly tugging at a lever on the dash that blows the whistle, and in those open-air cabs the noise was deafening. I had been given ear plugs for that reason, but discarded them after 10 or 15 minutes because I had trouble hearing what Kolkman and Willett were saying.

We were traveling through a rural area with a lot of grade crossings, some paved, but mostly dirt roads crossing the tracks. Kolkman blew the whistle at each and every one, even though from our elevated vantage point we could all see that there were no cars or trucks anywhere in sight. "You do it every time," he said. "No exceptions... ever."

Every engineer worries about hitting someone at one of those crossings. Kolkman said it hadn't happened to him, but many engineers have had to deal with it. It's a terrible experience, he said, and worse because there is almost nothing an engineer can do to prevent it. It simply takes too long to stop, and an automobile doesn't stand a chance in a collision with a moving train. "It's like running over a mailbox with your family car," he said.

Another hour went by quickly—too quickly for me—and we were now rattling along through farming country, with the pungent odor of manure coming and going as we passed fields that had recently been fertilized. After one particularly fragrant moment, Kolkman grinned and said, "Around here we say that's the smell of money."

Leaving Wisconsin Dells, the *Empire Builder* swung more to the west, heading almost directly into the setting sun. Next came Tomah and then La Crosse. Soon we were in Minnesota, running along the Mississippi River in the gathering darkness.

A freight train approached and Kolkman switched off the *Builder's* powerful headlight until the engines passed, then flipped it on again so he could visually inspect our side of the freight, looking for any sign of dragging equipment or a wheel or bearing problem. The radio in the cab crackled and we heard the voice of the freight train's engineer: "Looking good this side, Amtrak." "Thank you, sir," Kolkman responded, "Good run-by for you, too. Have a safe trip."

Twenty minutes later, the *Empire Builder* eased to a stop in Winona, Minnesota, and my cab ride was over. Bob Kolkman would continue to St. Paul where the next engineer would be boarding; Craig Willett was unsure how Amtrak planned to get him back to Milwaukee, but seemed unconcerned.

We all shook hands, I extracted a promise to let me know should either of them get to Hawaii, and climbed down out of the cab. The twin locomotives had stopped well beyond the Winona station's platform and my shoes crunched on the gravel ballast as I headed back to my sleeping car.

Later, after dinner and a hot shower, I remember lying in my berth as the black outlines of trees and lights from an occasional farmhouse flashed by outside my darkened compartment. In my mind's eye, I was now able to visualize quite clearly the new engineer methodically performing his routine up there in the head end of Amtrak locomotive number 343.

23

A Train Whistle Mystery

Travel by train around the United States and, if you're paying attention, you'll soon notice that Amtrak engineers blow the whistle quite a lot. And if you're *really* paying attention, you'll notice that there are several different whistle patterns—for example, two short toots when the train is about to move forward; three toots when it's about to back up.

By far the most common whistle signal is the one you hear every time the train approaches a grade crossing, which is where motor vehicles drive across the track: long-long-short-long. There will be minor variations—sometimes it's brisk, sometimes long and drawn out—depending on how fast the train is approaching the crossing. And sometimes you can detect a slight difference in the signal after a new engineer with a slightly different "touch" has come aboard in a crew change. But the signal itself is always the same: long-long-short-long. Furthermore, that's the way it's actually specified in railroad manuals.

But here's what I find so curious: no one seems to know where long-long-short-long came from. Over the years, I've asked many Amtrak people, including veteran conductors and engineers. *No one knows!*

Then, the other day, I got an email from a reader who said it's actually Morse Code for the letter "Q". (And indeed it is: dah-dah-dit-dah.) He went on to say he was told that British ships in the late 1800s blew long-long-short-long on the ship's horn—the letter "Q"—as a way of letting other maritime traffic know that Queen Victoria was on board and to yield the right of way. Certainly an interesting explanation... and, I thought, plausible, too.

To perhaps corroborate that explanation, I contacted Mark Smith, founder and the person behind *The Man in Seat 61*, by far the best and most complete web site devoted to rail travel anywhere in the world. As an expert on passenger rail and as a Brit, I could think of no one better to ask. Here is his response:

"The Queen story sounds apocryphal to me—though Queen Vic's reign up to 1901 would be the right time for railroading in the US to be starting and expanding, so Q... makes (some) sense."

So it's *possible* that the long-long-short-long whistle signal is actually "Q" for Queen. But somewhere... some time ago... someone made the decision that trains in North America—both passenger and freight—would blow long-long-short-long when approaching grade crossings. But who? And why that specific pattern? Does anyone know?

24

Parlez-vous American?

Ten years ago, while visiting friends in Norway, I accepted an invitation to speak to several high school classes. These boys and girls were ready to move on to the University level and, of course, they had already been learning English for probably 10 years.

One of the kids asked me an excellent question. Why is it, he wanted to know, that so few Americans speak another language?

I told them that fewer than half of American adults have passports and—this was an educated guess, of course—I thought the most likely reason that a large majority of those people have a passport is because one is now required to cross the border into either Canada or Mexico. Therefore, it's fair to assume that a much smaller percentage of Americans have passports because they plan to travel to Europe or Asia. For the purpose of this discussion, I said, it's a fact that more than half of all American adults do *not* have passports, which means they can't travel to foreign countries and, consequently, there is no need to learn a foreign language.

Those Norwegian kids were shocked.

The shameful fact is, it's probably safe to say that three-quarters of the U.S. population will never be exposed to other cultures or visit other countries where they might see something being done differently or—dare I say it?—done better than we do it in the U.S.

Now, can you guess which states rank lowest in terms of how many of their citizens own passports? Sure you can. In eight states, all in the south and the west, only about 25-percent of registered voters own passports. There are multiple implications to all of this.

Here's just one: If you can't travel outside the country, you have no way of knowing what it's like for ordinary people to have access to really good transportation systems or to appreciate the mobility and other benefits those systems provide.

In fact, it's not that much of a stretch to say we can attribute at least some of the opposition and most of the indifference to high speed rail to the fact that—a conservative guess—probably 95 percent of our adult population has never experienced an attendant casually pouring hot coffee for you on a train traveling 200 miles-per-hour.

Pretty damn discouraging, isn't it!

25

The Flåm Railway—Short, But Very Sweet

Several years ago, I visited a Norwegian couple I had met during my trans-Siberian trip. This time, I met them in Oslo and the three of us took the weekend to visit the small community of Flåm. The town's appeal is two-fold: it's located on a magnificent fjord and you get to Flåm on what has to be one of the most spectacular scenic railway lines in the world.

From Oslo, it was about a three-hour train ride to the little town of Myrdal—really nothing much more than a small station. From there, it's just a 20-mile ride down the mountain to Flåm, but while passing numerous waterfalls, the train sometimes clings to the side of the mountain, sometimes bores through some 20 tunnels.

Two-thirds of the way down, the train emerges from a tunnel and you're treated to a magnificent view of some of the tidy farms in the valley below. The village of Flåm is another five miles up ahead.

Besides the railway station, there's not much in the village itself: a hotel, a few guest houses, a couple of restaurants and two shops which feature whole aisles of what is clearly the most popular souvenir item: trolls.

The cruise on the fjord was amazing. Except when there were wakes from occasional passing boats, the water was perfectly still, producing mirror-like reflections of the steep cliffs on either side. Our ride was in the early morning and a number of wispy clouds still hung over the water which, we were told, was more than a thousand feet deep where we were cruising.

Bottom line: the Flåm Railway was the highlight of the whole trip.

26

James MacArthur
1937-2010

I turned on the computer this morning (October 31, 2010) and was hit with a news item reporting the death of actor James MacArthur.

Years ago, when the original *Hawaii 5-0* with Jack Lord as Steve McGarrett was being shot in and around Honolulu, I got to know Jimmy. His wife and mine were friends and we all hung out a bit together.

I had just started a small advertising agency and one of our clients was a small bank with just two branches. Nevertheless, they had aspirations for expansion, and we decided to produce a couple of 30-second television spots. I very hesitantly approached Jimmy to ask if he would appear in the commercials. To my delight, he immediately agreed and, when I asked about his fee, he waved his hand dismissively and said he would do it if the bank would replace the old television set in his Waikiki condo. It was a big, very generous, personal favor to me, of course.

The production was scheduled for a Saturday morning several weeks later when the two branches were closed for the weekend and normal bank operations wouldn't be disrupted.

We shot one commercial at the downtown branch in the morning, and moved on to the suburban branch that afternoon. Through it all, Jimmy MacArthur cheerfully endured all the inevitable re-takes and other delays for sound checks and lighting changes. He apologized when he fluffed a line and chatted amiably with the crew during the catered lunch. He was, in a word, the consummate professional and a joy to be around.

We finally finished shooting at 3:30 that afternoon, and his wife came to take him home. That was when I learned that Jimmy had been skiing in Colorado the week before and, because of blizzard conditions throughout that whole area, there were no flights in or out of Vail. As a result, he rented a car and drove 130 miles through the snow to the Denver airport. His flight to Los Angeles was delayed causing him to miss his connecting flight at LAX for Honolulu.

He had, in fact, arrived back in Honolulu at 5:00 that very morning, giving him just enough time to run home directly from the airport, shower and shave, have some breakfast, and get to the bank in time for the videotaping of our two insignificant local commercials.

Ever since, whenever I read about the petulant, selfish, thoughtless behavior of some of these prima donnas in sports or theater or business, I think of James Gordon MacArthur... who shames them all.

Book 'em, Danno!

THE BETTER TO SEE STUFF

VIA Rail's flagship—Train # 1, the west-bound Canadian—gets its windows washed during a 90-minute stop in Jasper, Alberta. The remainder of this day will take the train westward—deeper into the mountains, skirting the base of Mount Robson. At 12,972 feet, it's the tallest mountain in the Canadian Rockies. Tomorrow? Journey's end: Vancouver. (Jim Loomis photo)

27

Frank Fasi: Mayor and Golf Instructor

Frank Fasi was Mayor of Honolulu for 22 years. I'd like to believe he was elected and re-elected five times because of his many accomplishments... and surely they were a huge factor. But Frank was always in the news and often for unusual reasons. For instance, there was the time he landed a role in an episode of the original *Hawaii Five-O* television series.

It started late one afternoon when the filming of a scene for an episode caused a traffic jam on one of the major city streets in Honolulu. Mayor Fasi, who happened to be caught in the unusual congestion, pulled over and got out of his car to investigate. One glance was enough: the *Hawaii 5-0* cameras had been moved to the middle of the right-hand lane to get a better angle for one of the scenes being shot that afternoon. However, it effectively blocked one entire lane of a major street during rush hour. The mayor was irate.

The production crew was made up of local residents and they had recognized the mayor immediately. They were unable to warn the director before he had threatened to have the angry motorist arrested. The incident made the local media to the delight of general public and to the distress of the *Five-O* publicity department.

A week or so later, I got a call in my City Hall office from the *Five-O* casting director, Bob Busch, with what was obviously a peace offering. Bob said *Five-O* would be shooting a scene with Jack Lord on the Waialae Country Club golf course and they needed a couple of extras to be part of Steve McGarrett's foursome (McGarrett was the main character in the series played, of course, by Jack Lord). Would the mayor, asked Bob, be interested in being in the scene and would I like to come along, too?

Frank agreed and at the appointed time, we showed up at the golf course to find that one of the practice greens had been commandeered by the *Five-0* production crew. The director—this was not the same person who had caused the infamous traffic jam—described the scene we were about to shoot: while playing golf with the Mayor of Honolulu, Steve McGarrett would be interrupted by a phone call and have to dash off to deal with a development in an important case.

When everything was ready for the scene, Jack Lord emerged from his trailer, said hello, and began to rehearse the shot. The phone call was to come just as McGarrett was about to attempt a putt. Lord bent over the ball and gripped his putter when, startling everyone, the mayor suddenly said, "Hold it!"

Frank said from the way Jack Lord gripped the putter, every golfer in the TV audience would know that Steve McGarrett was *not* a golfer. And so, for the next couple of minutes, while the rest of the cast and crew watched nervously, my boss instructed Jack Lord on how to sink a short putt.

Finally Frank was satisfied and we all took our places. The director cried "Action!" Steve McGarrett sank his putt with passable form, his mobile phone rang right on cue, and he announced there had been a development that he would have to leave. Whereupon, with no notice and to everyone's surprise, the mayor ad libbed:

"Doggone it, Steve, I finally get you on the golf course and I'm beating you, and you have to leave!"

The director hollered "Cut!" and there were howls of laughter and applause. What's more, when that episode was edited, the Mayor's line was kept in the final cut that by now has been broadcast coast-to-coast and around the world many times.

Hawaii Five-0 reruns are still being shown here and there, and who knows? One of these nights when you can't sleep, you might actually catch the episode with that scene. If you do, look for the guy in the background holding the flag. That's me.

28

Traveling Abroad? Plan Carefully

I've always found travel—especially international travel—to be stimulating, interesting, and almost addicting. But it's too easy to relax, ignoring or forgetting what appear to be small details both in the planning and in the doing. Here's a kind of check list I've compiled over the years. The first three are particularly important and can avoid travel disruptions... even disasters.

1. ALWAYS have a back-up credit card when you travel. What if someone back home sees an unfamiliar charge on the current statement and asks your credit card company to check. If that perfectly legitimate phone call triggers a fraud alert, the only credit card in your wallet card could suddenly stop working just as you're about to check out of your hotel in Paris.

2. ALWAYS check the expiration date on your passport well in advance of your departure. Several foreign

countries will not honor a passport if it's going to expire less than six months in the future. Just imagine being prevented from boarding an international flight that was to be the start of a once-in-a-lifetime European vacation... a prepaid vacation. *Ouch!*

3. NEVER pack either your passport or your prescription medications in checked luggage. If your bag is lost or stolen or sent to Rome while you're headed to Oslo, you're screwed.

Here are three more, the consequences of which probably won't be all that serious, but will certainly be inconvenient:

4. MAKE SURE baggage tags are securely fastened to every piece of luggage and that the information on the tags is up-to-date and complete.

5. UPGRADE your smart phone service before you leave on a foreign trip with an international text, data, and voice plan. If you don't, once you leave the U.S., your smart phone will probably be useless.

6. BRING the right electrical adapters so you can charge your phone or use your computer and other electronic devices no matter what country you're in.

29

Local Politicians: Exhibits A and B

Hawaiian politics at the local level can produce some remarkable characters and, while I can't prove it, I'll bet that Hawaii probably has more than our fair share. Here are just two:

Frank Loo served on the Honolulu City Council for a number of years and was known for his unique way of campaigning. He would board a city bus, ride two or three blocks into his district, which was time enough to work his way to the back of the bus, greeting every passenger and offering one of his campaign brochures. Then he would get off the bus, cross the street, and catch the next bus heading back into his district. Other politicians walk door to door giving out campaign material; Frank Loo took the bus.

But Loo is primarily remembered for an incident that occurred during a City Council hearing on a proposed ordinance that would allow people—women, in particular—to carry pepper spray for self-protection.

When one of the witnesses, a middle-aged woman, testified in favor of the proposal, Councilman Loo expressed skepticism that pepper spray could effectively ward off a determined attacker.

The lady indignantly suggested that Loo could find out for himself by trying to attack her. Eager to meet any challenge, and very much aware that there were television cameras in the Council Chambers that day, Loo rose from his seat and rushed at the lady. She snatched a can of the pepper spray from her purse, waited until Councilman Loo was about to bear hug her, and to the delight of everyone present, gave him a snoot full of the spray, leaving him choking and gasping on the floor of the Council Chambers. The entire confrontation was the lead story on all three TV stations at both 6:00 and 10:00 that evening when it was revealed that Councilman Loo's female opponent that day was a member of the Women's Self-Defense League. How's *that* for a political legacy?

Richard Kageyama was always known as a bit of an eccentric. He served on the Honolulu Board of Supervisors, the City Council, and in the state legislature on and off for many years. When appearing before any kind of a public gathering, he would often begin his remarks with a resounding "Fello-o-o-o-w students..."

He thought it was funny and that it would amuse and relax his audience, but in the several times I saw him use that opener, the reaction was just confusion.

However, Kageyama did have a remarkably effective tactic

to win votes during his re-election campaigns. From the Public Works Department, he would obtain a schedule for all the street repairs in his Council district. On the day before work was scheduled to begin, he would go up and down the very street knocking on doors. When a resident appeared, Kageyama would introduce himself and say he had been walking through the district and couldn't help but notice that there were quite a few potholes in the street.

"Would you like me to get those fixed for you?" he would ask.

The startled homeowner would, of course, say yes, where-upon Kageyama would scribble something on a little notepad and say, "I'll have them here first thing tomorrow morning!"

Loo and Kageyama were both elected and re-elected by their constituents multiple times. The political pundits could never understand why.

30

The Case for Long Distance Trains

It had been a lousy day and not a good beginning for a trip to Chicago for a three-day meeting. Just getting to L.A. from Maui had involved a cancelled flight, several hours sitting in the Maui airport, and no room in First Class on the next plane despite having a first-class ticket. And, of course, there was a very late arrival into Los Angeles.

But the view from the 16th floor of the Hilton at LAX was spectacular, if not sobering. I stood at the window for several minutes after waking up, watching planes landing one after another at the rate of one every 90 seconds and remembering it had been the same the previous Spring at JFK and at London's Heathrow. The skies are crowded almost everywhere, and flying hasn't been a pleasant experience for decades.

I caught the 10 o'clock shuttle bus for downtown Los Angeles, got off at Union Station and, after leaving my bag in Amtrak's first-class lounge, walked two blocks up to Olivera Street. It's famous for dozens of shops selling everything from fine art to cheap souvenirs, all with authentic Mexican themes. But there are also several really excellent Mexican restaurants and at one of these I met a former client for a long, delightful "catching-up" lunch.

By late afternoon, I was back at Union Station and settled in a comfortable chair in Amtrak's first-class lounge, reviewing emails until time to board Train #4, the *Southwest Chief.*

It was an on-time departure at 6:00 p.m. and first call for dinner in the dining car came 40 minutes later. I ordered the steak with a baked potato and a half bottle of merlot to go with it.

My dinner companions that night were a personable graduate student in Engineering, returning to his studies at the University of Kansas at Lawrence, and an interesting couple from Ireland. He was a poet with several published books of his work, while she was an executive with a health care organization. She is not impressed by our health care system.

This was "community dining" at its best, and meeting interesting fellow passengers is without doubt what I have come to enjoy most about Amtrak's long-distance train travel.

After dinner, I returned to my roomette to find that the car attendant had made up my berth and, after a hot shower, I climbed into bed. About the time the Chief was halfway between Barstow and Needles, I drifted off to sleep listening to some of my favorite Hawaiian music.

The next day brought more changes to the passing scenery as the *Chief* cut across the bottom corner of Colorado following the original Santa Fe Trail, parts of which are still visible alongside the tracks. In mid-morning, we came upon four mounted cowboys loading a dozen cows into a truck. They paused and gazed at us as we slowly rolled by. And one, responding, I suppose, to a wave from one of our female passengers, reached up and in a magnificently underplayed gesture, nodded and touched the brim of his Stetson.

At lunch, I shared my table in the dining car with a mother and daughter going to Kansas City where the daughter's husband had been undergoing treatment for a rare medical condition. He was much improved and, after spending two days in Kansas City, this same train will bring the three of them back to their home near Flagstaff, Arizona. The young man and his wife will travel in an "accessible bedroom." Designed to transport medical patients and an attendant, there's one in every Superliner sleeping car.

I left the *Southwest Chief* around noon the following day when the train stopped in Galesburg, Illinois. My brother, Pete, and his wife live just 15 minutes away in the town of Monmouth. The three of us caught up on family news that night over a nice dinner at their favorite restaurant.

The next morning, Pete drove me back to the railroad station in Galesburg, where I caught Amtrak's train, the *Carl Sandburg,* for the three-hour ride into Chicago.

And now, finally, we get to my reason for taking you through some of the highlights of my journey from Los Angeles to Chicago on the *Southwest Chief.* It is to suggest that, in the grand scheme of things, Amtrak is in many ways a better choice for long-distance travel than flying.

As a matter of fact, how do most of us *really* feel about air travel these days? Yes, it's all very impressive, but as passengers, are we happy with how we're treated? Or have we been bullied into accepting treatment that would be unacceptable anywhere else.

Most train stations are conveniently located in the middle of the city; airports are often 25 miles out of town. We hand over our personal belongings to be inspected and even searched. We are squeezed into narrow seats that won't recline and have no leg room. And the food? Well, let me just say that the infamous "turkey wrap" offered on a major U.S. airline cannot compare to a "signature steak" in an Amtrak dining car.

Passenger trains are the only civilized way left for travel and are far better for the environment. So may I humbly suggest that the next time the prospect of some travel comes up, don't just automatically assume you'll fly. Instead, think about taking the train.

31

Red Sox Nation

If you grew up in New England, there's about a 95 percent chance that you are a fan of the Boston Red Sox. Perhaps there's something in the water, but there are no fans anywhere as knowledgeable, as passionate, or as loyal.

For me, it all started on the 25th of May in 1946. I had been invited to spend the weekend in Boston with my mother's younger sister, who had a summer job there. Aunt Bobby took me to Fenway Park to see the Red Sox play the New York Yankees, so it's all her fault!

I can still remember the crowd pressing to get into Fenway Park, shuffling down a long ramp into the dank, dark bowels of the ballpark, spotting the sign indicating the section where our seats were located, heading up another ramp and finally emerging into the dazzling afternoon sunlight and my first ever look at the manicured playing field.

I don't remember anything specific about the game itself, except that the Red Sox defeated the Yankees that afternoon.

The score was 7-4 and I know that for a fact because I have the box score of the game framed and on my desk.

Wear a Boston Red Sox cap or T-shirt anywhere—and I mean literally anywhere in the world—and sooner or later you will get a nod or a grin or a handshake or even a spontaneous conversation from someone else who shares the same passion for that baseball team. It seems to happen a lot in railway stations. Four that I remember off hand: Sienna, Berlin, St. Petersburg (in Russia) and Gare de Montparnasse in Paris.

Before taking the trans-continental train ride across Australia on the *Indian Pacific,* I was wearing my Red Sox cap as I strolled around Sydney for a couple of days. Twice I was greeted with a cheery "Go Sox" from other sightseers and once by a muttered "Red Sox suck!" from a passing cretin, clearly a fan of the New York Yankees.

In the lounge car of Amtrak's *Southwest Chief,* I was hailed by a Japanese doctor who had spotted the distinctive red B on the pocket of my polo shirt. He had just completed a two-year program at one of the Boston hospitals, during which time he had become a rabid and very knowledgeable Red Sox fan. We shared a table that night in the dining car.

Our personal financial advisor, Itaat Husain, is originally from Pakistan and is a passionate Red Sox fan. For my birthday a few years back, he gave me a baseball autographed by Carl Yastrzemski, thus making our relationship a lifetime appointment.

When my wife and I retired to Maui, I had to find a primary care physician. From the list of 40 or more doctors at the Maui Medical Group, I picked a Dr. Mitchell purely at random. It turned out he went to medical school in Boston where he became a passionate Red Sox fan. His nurses tell me they have learned to schedule an extra five minutes for my appointments to allow doctor and patient to discuss the latest news from Fenway Park.

But the weirdest experience so far occurred probably 20 years ago in the town of Pécs in the south of Hungary. My wife and I were on our way to browse through the town's weekly outdoor market when I noticed a battered old Skoda–the eastern bloc equivalent of a VW beetle–parked on a side street. There was a huge decal almost filling the entire rear window:

BOSTON RED SOX
1986 American League Champions

I hung around the car for a while, hoping the owner would show up, but to my everlasting disappointment, he never did. The two of us would have had a lot to talk about because 1986 was the year the Sox played the New York Mets in the World Series and Bill Buckner made a critical error in Game Six and... Well, we would have had a lot to talk about.

32

A Baseball Mystery Solved on the Chief

Ralph Branca was on the mound for the Brooklyn Dodgers in the Fall of 1951 for the deciding game with the New York Giants to determine who would be the National League champions and play the Yankees in the World Series. In the bottom of the 9th inning, the game was decided when Giants outfielder Bobby Thompson hit a home run—forever to be known as "the shot heard 'round the world".

Twenty or so years ago, I took Amtrak's *Southwest Chief* from Los Angeles to Kansas City to see the Boston Red Sox in a three-game series with the Royals. On the return ride to L.A., I was having dinner in the dining car and one of my tablemates was an older lady from New York City.

We went through the usual where-are-you-going ice breakers and when she learned that I was a serious baseball fan, she said, "I have a story about baseball I think will interest you."

It seems her father was the chief electrician at the Polo

Grounds in New York, which was the home ballpark of the New York Giants baseball team before they left for San Francisco in 1958.

One evening in September of 1951, the lady said, her father came home from work and, over dinner, remarked that he had been directed to install some new wiring in the centerfield scoreboard. She said her father described the wiring as "suspicious" and he speculated that it could be used as a signaling system. That is, someone inside the scoreboard with powerful binoculars could see the signals flashed by the opposing team's catcher to his pitcher. The new wiring could be used to turn on and off a small light on the front of the scoreboard in a manner that would let the batter know if he should be looking for a curveball.

Ever since that memorable game in 1951 and Bobby Thompson's game-winning homer, there has been speculation that he knew what kind of pitch was coming. He and the Giants management have always denied it, but the rumor had never gone away—not even after more than a half-century.

But there I was, somewhere east of Gallup, New Mexico, in an Amtrak dining car, finding out that the old rumor was probably true. As Mel Allen would say, How about that!*

---

* Bobby Thompson died August 16, 2010. He was 86. Ralph Branca died on November 23, 2016. He was 90.

33

The Emperor Comes to Honolulu

In October of 1975, Emperor Hirohito of Japan arrived in Honolulu, the last stop of an official state visit to the United States. Frank Fasi was Honolulu's mayor at that time, and the governor was George Ariyoshi. The two were bitter political rivals, but it had been agreed that each man would host a formal event of some kind for the emperor.

Gov. Ariyoshi and his advisors decided on a luncheon for the emperor and empress at Washington Place, the governor's official residence. And of course, Governor Ariyoshi's guest list included all his political cronies and major supporters. Unimaginative, but entirely predictable.

Mayor Fasi, on the other hand, decided to stage a program of entertainment for Hirohito, with local performers representing all the various ethnicities we have here in Hawaii. The Royal Hawaiian Band played the national anthems; there was Hawaiian music and hula, the Honolulu City Ballet, Filipino *tinikling* performers, a Samoan knife dancer, and several other ethnic groups entertained.

But to generate his guest list, Mayor Fasi had invitations sent to 9,000 Oahu residents—every 10th name on the list of people with a Hawaii driver's license. And so, in addition to seeing a sample of Hawaii's various cultures, the emperor and empress would see—and be seen by—an almost perfect cross-section of Honolulu's multi-ethnic, multi-racial population.

The U.S. Secret Service was providing security for the emperor while he was in this country and Frank's idea for a guest list was a security nightmare. As it happened, I was the one who informed the Secret Service agent in charge that we were going to invite several thousand randomly selected local residents to the mayor's event. I can quote his reaction exactly: "Oh, shit!" But then he said, "Well, it's your party and we work for you. So we'll deal with it."

The emperor's visit took place on schedule and, happily, it all went off without incident. The mayor's event was a huge success, with a good deal of national media coverage, some of which include a reference to how the audience had been selected.

Protocol required that the mayor and his wife, Joyce, be included as guests at Governor Ariyoshi's luncheon. By chance, I happened to be in his office when Frank returned from that event. He said it was very formal and quite stiff. And then he said that the seats assigned to him and Joyce had been at the far end of one of the tables with their backs to the head table and facing the swinging doors through which all the food was brought in from the kitchen. The mayor and his wife had deliberately been assigned the two worst seats in the room.

I was incensed at what was obviously a calculated effort to demean the mayor of the 11th largest municipal government in the United States and I offered to let several of the media people know about it. Frank just waved it off, however, saying that it would just be a note of pettiness injected into what was otherwise quite a splendid day. He was right, of course.

WIND-POWER AT WORK

Aboard Amtrak's east bound *Sunset Limited* we have already passed what seemed to be hundreds of these giant wind turbines apparently placed at random throughout the area. This one row of turbines stretches clear across the valley east of Palm Springs, California. Here, as the terrain narrows into a natural funnel, we pass a wall of about 30 of the devices. (Jim Loomis photo)

34

Fashion Trends, Hawaii-Style

One of Hawaii's many gifts to the rest of the United States, and indeed to much of the rest of the world, is what we refer to as "aloha wear", which is a reference to the shirts and long dresses (*"muumuu"*) most made from the colorful floral prints traditionally worn here. Mainland people are often surprised to discover that aloha shirts are considered appropriate business attire for men in Hawaii, as are ladies' blouses and dresses of the same colorful fabrics. There is one important proviso for the men, however: the shirts must be tucked in. Aloha shirts worn out? Well, that's fine for any informal situation, but it's not accepted business attire.

By no means was it always this way. In 1962, when I first arrived in Honolulu, local businessmen dressed quite conservatively. That meant business suits, although they were usually made of lightweight fabrics suitable for the tropics... seersucker, for example. And one would also see suits and sports jackets in lighter shades of color.

Then one day—I think it was probably in the early 1970's—a delegation from Hawaii's garment industry made an appointment to see Honolulu's mayor, Frank Fasi. They came with a request: would the mayor consider issuing a proclamation designating the last day of every work week between Memorial Day and Labor Day as *Aloha Friday* and declaring that aloha wear—that is, aloha shirts and muumuus—would be considered appropriate business attire on those specific days?

Understanding that it would be helpful to the local garment industry, Mayor Fasi was happy to oblige. And so, Aloha Friday was born. Of course, a mayoral proclamation has no legal standing whatsoever; nevertheless, Aloha Fridays became an instant success, with men and women at almost every level in the local economy buying new aloha shirts and muumuus.

A few years later, another delegation from the garment industry paid a visit to the mayor, requesting yet another proclamation—but this time it was to create *Aloha Summer*, which would proclaim aloha shirts and muumuus as acceptable attire for *every* business day, five days a week, between Memorial Day and Labor Day.

Once again, the mayor was glad to oblige, another proclamation was issued, and *Aloha Summer* became part of life in Hawaii.*

It was inevitable, of course, that a few years after that, Labor Day came and went, but the aloha shirts remained. Since then, aloha wear is considered acceptable business attire for every day, year 'round... but only if the shirts are tucked in.

---

* One exception remains: court officials—attorneys and prosecutors—are required to wear business suits with dress shirts and ties for court appearances.

35

Signs of the Times

For much of my trip to Russia and China in 2011, I was in a group with local guides. That was easy... comfortable. All you have to do is pay attention and listen for instructions and not get separated from the group.

But I was traveling on my own for almost two weeks before joining the group in Moscow and the fact is, no matter where you travel you depend on signs to get you where you need to go: to a public bathroom, to a scenic lookout, to the railway station, to your train.

Icons help a lot, and in France or Italy or Germany or Switzerland much of the time the words on the signs look like the corresponding word in English. In Milan, you know you're going to get something to eat when the sign over the door says "Ristorante".

Chinese characters pose a problem, of course, but a lot of the signs in China—in fact, most of those that would be helpful to foreigners—are also in English. You get the information you need, even if the translation isn't always quite right.

I found it much more difficult in Russia where the signs all use the Cyrillic alphabet. There is simply no connection, and I remember thinking that my experience in Russia must be what it feels like to be illiterate. You find yourself almost desperately looking for other clues... icons, for example.

It can be disconcerting to check on your train in railway stations if you can't recognize the Cyrillic spelling of your destination city and the departure time for your train has changed. In that case, you had damn well better know the train number!

It's particularly worrisome when the design or the layout of the sign gives the impression that its message is important. Big red letters with lightning bolts or multiple exclamation points. That's when you sharpen your instincts and, in particular, pay attention to what everyone around you is doing. Or not doing.

I confess that I took a stab at learning the Cyrillic alphabet before I left on that trip, but gave up after a few half-hearted sessions. I did find the perfect solution for getting around St. Petersburg. I hired my own guide. Her name was Natasha, and she had her own car. Trust me: It's the only way to go!

36

The Glacier Express: A Head End Ride

My approach to things that seem unattainable at first blush is simply to ask—the theory being, the worst possible result is that someone will say, "No." And so, when planning a European trip for 2015, I emailed the Swiss Tourism Office and asked if I could get an hour-long ride in the head end on the Glacier Express. *And they said yes!*

The Glacier Express is operated by the Rhaetian Railway and runs between St. Moritz and Zermatt in Switzerland. There is one train a day in the winter months and three a day during the summer. On this trip, I boarded in Chur and, by prior arrangement, was escorted up to the head end at Andermat for the hour and a half ride to Brig.

Much of the scenery is breathtakingly beautiful, with farmhouses scattered up and down the verdant Alpine slopes. The windows in the train are huge and spotlessly clean, which is of course what you would expect from the Swiss.

The engineer—they refer to him as the driver—spoke no

English and was a man of few words anyway, even with a representative from the railroad with us to translate.

In a way, the Glacier Express is a misnomer, because our speed on straight, flat stretches (which are few and far between) topped out at about 40 mph. The windows in the head end are also huge and I had a great view from the left hand seat.

As expected, the train makes some steep climbs and descents along its route and is assisted in both the ups and downs by a gear-like device beneath the locomotive that locks into the special track between the two rails in those areas. Technically, I believe it's a rack and pinion system, and without it, this train would quickly lose traction.

The Rhaetian Railway also operates the Bernina Express, which crosses into Italy, terminating at the town of Tirano. Both are great rides, but my personal opinion is that the Bernina Express is the better of the two. Best idea: do both!

37

The Proof is in the Parking Lot

In December of 1978, I had just been named General Manager of the Hawaii Islanders, Honolulu's minor league baseball team in the Pacific Coast League. At that time, the Islanders were the Triple-A farm team for the San Diego Padres, who provided our players. Ray Kroc, founder of the McDonald's hamburger empire, had bought the Padres four years earlier.

My first official duty as the new Islander GM was to attend the annual baseball Winter Meetings, which were held that year in Orlando, Florida. I flew to San Diego where I joined a lot of other people who either worked for the Padres or for one of the minor league teams connected to the organization. Together, as a group, we flew from San Diego to Orlando on the Padre's private jet.

After landing in Orlando, we all boarded a chartered bus that was waiting to take us directly to the hotel in downtown

Orlando where we were staying and where the meetings would be starting the next day.

I was in a window seat toward the front of the bus and who should climb aboard and plunk down in the seat next to me, but Ray Kroc himself. I introduced myself as the bus left the airport and headed off into the city.

About twenty minutes later, and in the middle of a very pleasant conversation, Ray Kroc suddenly lurched to his feet and lunged in front of me, pressing his nose against the bus window. It took me a few seconds, but I realized that we were, at that moment, passing a McDonald's restaurant... and Ray Kroc, founder and chairman of the board of the McDonald's hamburger empire, was counting the cars in the parking lot.

After a few seconds, he sat down, scowled at me and grumbled, "There should be more cars this time of day!" He fished around in his coat pocket for a small notepad and a pen, scribbled a few words on a blank page, and muttered, "I gotta call the manager of that store."

And now we know how McDonald's has managed to sell all those Big Macs.

MAKE WAY, PLEASE

The sightseeing domes on most of VIA Rail's long distance western trains offer passengers some spectacular views of the Canadian scenery and, for train travel enthusiasts, a close look at a passing freight train every so often is a real treat, especially from a seat in the dome car. But the tracks are owned by Canadian National Railway and their trains are given priority. That, unfortunately, means VIA Rail trains, each with several hundred passengers, are forced to sit and wait on sidings while CN freights rumble by. (Jim Loomis photo)

38

Think About a Personal Tour Guide

I love to travel, but I hate being a tourist. Most especially, I don't like being one of 50 or 60 tourists going from one historic site to another in a bus. A gaggle of people, piling off the bus, gawking at whatever it is we're there to see. It just seems so intrusive. Small groups are preferred. The smaller the better, in fact.

In the Fall of 2013, I took a tour of the Normandy beaches in France. It was in a van with a driver—just a half dozen people, all interested and respectful. And we had an articulate and knowledgeable guide. Very much worth the time and the money.

But if a place is worth traveling halfway around the world to see, shouldn't we get the most we can out of the experience? For me, that means getting a real "feel" for a place... learning something about what it's like to actually live there. And, clearly, the best way to do that is to hire your own personal guide. I've done that in St. Petersburg, in Shanghai, in Siena and last year in Ypres.

These guides are licensed, all very knowledgable, and they're known to the people running the historical sites. My guide in Siena was a delightful young woman named Costanza. Smart, fluent in English, and a font of information about that wonderful city and the surrounding region. And she also knew where to find the very best gelato in all of Siena. Two years earlier, it was Jean in Shanghai and Natasha in St. Petersburg—the first day in the city, the second for a trip to the Czar's Summer Palace.

Yes, of course a personal guide is more expensive. It varies, but it cost me $200 for a six-hour tour that would probably be $60 per person on a bus with 30 or 40 other people. For my two days with Natasha in St. Petersburg, we communicated ahead of time by email so she knew that I was more interested in learning about the terrible 1,000-day siege of the city by the German army in World War 2 than visiting three or four Russian Orthodox cathedrals with 50 other tourists.

And, because I'm interested in day-to-day life of the local people in all these cities, I emailed the guides ahead of time that I would like them to plan for a pleasant leisurely lunch at a restaurant serving very good authentic local food which will allow plenty of time for the two of us to chat about contemporary life in their cities.

My point here is to ask who got better value for their money? Was it the visitors who saw St. Petersburg with a busload of 50 other people? Or was it me, able to take however much time I wanted to visit sites in which I was specifically interested and hearing about the lives of local residents in one-on-one informal conversations over a nice meal with an intelligent, informed local resident?

After having opted for private guides in St. Petersburg, Shanghai, and Siena—and considering the amount of time and money it took to get me there all the way from Hawaii—I do believe it was a much better choice than the typical bus tour.

Finding a personal guide is easy. Go to TripAdvisor and type in "tour guide" and the name of the city or town. There will probably be several listed along with some information about each person and some reviews, too. And before you ask what their fee is, remind yourself what it's going to cost to get you there from your hometown.

39

Hungary: Before and After the Russians

Back in the mid-80s, my wife and I made the first of two trips to Hungary. We took an overnight train from Paris to Vienna then, two days later, another train for the four-hour ride to Budapest.

When our train stopped at the Austro-Hungarian border, uniformed Hungarian military personnel boarded and moved slowly from car to car, checking everyone's tickets and papers. When two armed soldiers reached our compartment, they gestured for us to step out into the corridor.

While we stood there, one of them carefully examined our tickets and passports and asked a series of questions: What business did we have in Hungary? Where were we staying? Did we have any Hungarian friends? Were we bringing any gifts with us? Did we have any books or magazines? (A young man in the next compartment had his PLAYBOY magazine confiscated.)

Meanwhile, the other soldier was inside our compartment,

lifting up the seat cushions and, with a flashlight, peering up into the crawl space above the ceiling to make sure no one was hiding there.

Outside, a soldier was stationed opposite the vestibules of each car on both sides of the train. Two other soldiers slowly worked their way down the length of the train—one with a large dog on a leash, the other with a mirror on the end of a long pole which he held under each car, obviously looking for someone who might be clinging to the underside of one of the rail cars. The whole process took about an hour and was, I assure you, a sobering experience. When the train finally started moving, I felt a palpable sense of relief.

But times change. Just a dozen years later, we made a second trip to Hungary, this time after glasnost had come to Russia and the entire Eastern bloc. Once again our train paused at the border where, as before, two uniformed Hungarians came through the train. No guns... cheerful... asked a couple of questions... glanced at our passports and said, "Please enjoy your visit."

By coincidence, the very first McDonalds restaurant had opened in Budapest less than a week before our arrival. We passed it on the way to our hotel and saw long lines of customers spilling out onto the street.

Later that night, we asked some Hungarian friends if they had been to the McDonalds yet and, if so, what did they think of it.

"Well," said Istvan, "the food was wonderful, of course, but *so expensive!*"

I thought about that comment for days, even after we had left Hungary. At home, we eat at McDonald's because the food is totally predictable and it's fast and cheap. Istvan loved the food at McDonald's, but could only afford to go there for special occasions. The world is upside-down!

CARCASSONNE

In the 5th century, after many years of being sacked by warring armies, this French town turned itself into a fortified city with a drawbridge and 53 towers, all built over a period of many years. The amazing thing to consider is the amount of simple human effort that must have gone into the huge complex. (Jim Loomis photo)

40

Daniel K. Inouye
1924-2012

It's simply not possible for someone who isn't from Hawaii to fully understand the respect and esteem in which Senator Dan Inouye was held by his constituents here. Hawaii's senior senator was very low-key, but in a system that equates seniority with power, Inouye had influence almost beyond measure. He served as a United States senator for more than 50 years.

When the Navy's famous battleship *Missouri* was about to be permanently decommissioned, it was berthed at the

Navy base in Bellingham, Washington. Recognizing the great ship's place in the country's history, the city fathers there put together a professional marketing presentation to convince the Navy that the Missouri, when decommissioned, should be permanently berthed in Bellingham and converted into a floating museum.

Meantime, people in Honolulu felt that the *Missouri's* permanent home should be at Pearl Harbor. The surrender documents ending World War 2 had been signed in a ceremony on her deck in 1945, and as a floating museum in Pearl Harbor she would be moored near the battleship *Arizona*, lost on December 7, 1941, with more than 1,000 men still entombed within her sunken hull—two great ships serving as bookends for the greatest conflict in human history.

According to legend, a delegation from Hawaii went to Washington to ask the senior senator's help in convincing the Navy that the Missouri rightfully belonged at Pearl Harbor.

It was a brief meeting. Inouye immediately understood what they wanted. "No problem," he said, "I'll phone the admiral." Indeed, that's all it took—one phone call from Dan Inouye—and today the Mighty Mo is permanently anchored in Pearl Harbor.

It was hard to read Inouye's reaction to any discussion since his face didn't usually reveal his emotions. Once, back in the late '90s, I was in his office to shoot a TV spot in which the senator would endorse my friend and client, Neil Abercrombie, for re-election to the U.S. House.

While the crew was setting up their gear and fussing with the lighting, I was engaging the senator in conversation, hoping he wouldn't become impatient with the delays. After chatting about some of the current issues in the news, I said I was happy to see that he appeared to be in good health.

"Well," he said, "I try to stay in shape. And I feel pretty good."

He paused, and then he said, "Of course, a couple of months ago I fell in the shower and broke my arm."

I was surprised, but managed to say I was sorry to hear that.

He shrugged, then said, almost as an after-thought, "The amazing thing is, it's only eight inches long."

I was struck dumb because I had assumed he had broken his *left* arm, not the stump of the right one, the result of combat in Italy during World War 2 that had earned him the Medal of Honor. And so I stood staring, with no idea how to respond. Of course, nothing about his expression offered any help. Mercifully, at that very moment, the production crew took me off the hook by announcing we were ready to start shooting.

All these years later, that's my personal Dan Inouye story. It may not be much, but it's unique and it's kind of funny and it belongs only to me. And I'll always treasure it.

41

A Remarkable Safety Record

I take plenty of time planning my trips. For one thing, I enjoy that process—deciding where I want to go, how I'll get there, what there is to see and do there, and where to stay. I get little pleasure from flying, so I try to minimize my time in the air.

If Europe is the ultimate destination, I'll fly to one of the West Coast cities and take Amtrak from there to Washington or New York or Boston for a flight to London or Paris.

On the subject of flying, I had a conversation some time ago over a meal on VIA Rail traveling from Toronto to Vancouver. A woman at our table expressed the view that she would be wary of flying to Hawaii because it's such a long over-water flight. In fact, it's quite true that the flight from the West Coast of the U.S. to Hawaii is the longest over-water flight in the world without an alternate landing site.

So just how hazardous is it?

Answer: It's not. In fact, while a handful of flights have been forced to ditch for one reason or another, there have been only two serious incidents involving commercial aircraft carrying passengers.

The first occurred in 1956 when PanAm flight 6, en route to California from Honolulu, lost two of its four engines. When the pilot was certain they could not make landfall, he steered the Boeing *Stratocruiser* toward a Coast Guard ship permanently stationed near the halfway mark to provide a relaying service for radio messages between Hawaii and the U.S. mainland. Blessed with relatively calm seas, he made a textbook water landing and all passengers and crew survived.

A year later, PanAm flight 7, also a Boeing *Stratocruiser*, westbound to Honolulu, was lost with no survivors. After extensive hearings and several theories, including one that the plane had been sabotaged, the explanation as to the exact cause of flight 7s disappearance is still inconclusive.

Considering how many commercial flights there are between the West Coast and Hawaii just on a normal day, to have only two serious incidents since Day One—none involving a jet aircraft—is a testimony to the reliability and durability of today's modern aircraft and to the people who build and maintain them.

42

In Tahiti, Take Le Truck

I was enjoying some Tahitian music on one of the local radio stations earlier today and it brought back some wonderful memories of our several visits to that part of the world.

French Polynesia consists of several groups of islands, the better-known being Tahiti, with the capital city, Papeete. From Hawaii, Papeete is a six-hour, non-stop, once-a-week flight due south on Hawaiian Airlines. From Los Angeles, at this writing, flights to Tahiti are offered by United, Qantas and Air Tahiti. Other islands in French Polynesia with significant populations are Moorea, Bora Bora, Raiatea, and Huahine. It's an incredibly beautiful place with its own unique charm... each island offering an exotic blend of the authentic Polynesian with a thick veneer of French.

These islands also offer what has to be one of the most colorful and practical forms of public transportation anywhere: *le truck*. Essentially, these are small to mid-size trucks that have been modified with a wooden roof and partially open sides.

I'm sure that there are minimum specifications to which every vehicle must conform, but it's obvious from the variety of paint schemes that visual flexibility is permitted. And most of these wonderful vehicles have boom boxes mounted inside that are blaring Tahitian music.

Heading into Papeete for a doctor's appointment? Take *le truck*. Traveling to the far side of the island? Take *le truck*. When you're ready to go, just stand at the side of the road. *Le truck* will be along in a few minutes. Drivers are independent entrepreneurs, who follow specific routes and charge fares that are regulated by the government. Your fellow passengers will be a colorful and jovial mixture of the island population, often one or two visiting backpackers, and an occasional bank president from Indiana thrown in for good measure. You just never know.

Of course, with all the regulatory agencies and liability concerns in our litigious society, *le truck* would never work in the U.S. But, once again, somebody in a far corner of the world has come up with a wonderful, practical, efficient, economical public transit system. One that works.

43

Richard Nixon: All Tucked Out

Politics is a very, very tough business and it's a rare bird who can plunge deep into the world of big-time politics and still maintain some perspective and a sense of humor.

As a professional political consultant, Dick Tuck worked for some big-time races in the 1950s and 60s. But among a group of older political insiders, he's fondly remembered today for the stunts he dreamed up for the express purpose of causing heartburn for Richard Nixon.

On one occasion, during his campaign for governor of California, Nixon made an appearance before a crowd in San Francisco's Chinatown. Tuck arranged for a group of Chinese children to cheer and hold up welcoming signs with the message in Chinese characters. Ah, but the signs translated as *What About the Hughes Loan?*, a reference to an unsecured loan of $200,000 made to Nixon's brother by Howard Hughes. Nixon was not amused. When one of his supporters whispered the actual translation in his ear, Nixon grabbed one of the signs and tore it to pieces... on camera.

The day after the famous Nixon-Kennedy TV debate, Tuck hired a sweet little old lady, pinned a huge Nixon button on her, and had her approach Nixon at a campaign event. In front of all the cameras, she gave him a big hug, and said for all the world to hear: "Don't worry, son. He beat you last night, but you'll get him next time!"

Tuck switched roles and became a candidate himself years later when he ran for the California State Senate. He lost badly, and on election night he stepped to the microphone at his campaign headquarters and delivered the shortest and most memorable concession speech in the history of American politics:

"The people have spoken... *the bastards!*"

Dick Tuck retired to Arizona where he died in 2018 at age 94. Here's hoping his example may encourage this country to find a way to restore an occasional element of humor to our political campaigns.

44

The Cardinal Makes a Convert

Every so often, those of us who are advocates for passenger rail—specifically for long-distance trains—have the chance to see someone become a convert in front of our very eyes.

Some years back, I met a woman over lunch on Amtrak's train #51, the westbound Cardinal. I was heading for Chicago following a NARP meeting in Washington. She had some high-stress job in Philadelphia and was treating herself to several relaxing days at the famous Greenbrier resort in White Sulphur Springs, West Virginia.

I was shown to a seat across from her at lunch and almost from the moment I sat down, she started raving about her experience on the Cardinal. When she first got the idea for the luxurious getaway, her first thought was to fly. That is, until she discovered that it would involve two stops, almost five hours en route, and close to $800 for the round-trip air fare.

But someone had suggested she look into taking the train.

She did and was delighted with the experience. She had boarded the Cardinal in Philadelphia just after 8:00 that morning and would be at the Greenbrier in plenty of time for dinner.

In the meantime, she was positively crowing about having her own private accommodations and the lovely scenery—we had just crossed the Blue Ridge mountains. She was marveling at being able to get up and walk around, and about having a decent meal in the dining car. And all for a couple of hundred dollars less that it would have cost her to fly.

The big laugh came at the end of the meal when, not yet realizing that her meal was included in her fare, she tried to pay for her lunch. She was delighted, of course.

I can't tell you how many times I've gone through a version of that experience. You can almost see the light bulb go off when someone suddenly understands the difference between flying and taking an overnight train:

Your vacation begins when you get *off the plane*; but it starts when you get *on the train*.

By the way, have you ever wondered how Amtrak came to name this train The Cardinal? It's because when the train departs from Washington, DC, en route to Chicago, it passes through six states: Virginia, West Virginia, Kentucky, Ohio, Indiana and Illinois. And the cardinal is the official state bird for all six of them.

45

A Changing of the Gauge

My 2011 trip to Russia and China included rail travel from London to Berlin to Moscow to St. Petersburg and back to Moscow.

At that point, I joined a tour that took us by rail across Siberia to Mongolia, then down to Beijing. On my own once again there, I took the Chinese high-speed train to Shanghai, and flew home via Seoul. The trains involved varied in design and comfort quite a lot.

On the Russian train that took me overnight from Berlin to Moscow, moving from car to car through the vestibules took some careful footwork, while the passageway between the Chinese sleepers was actually carpeted. I must note that the interiors of the two cars were both very acceptable, although the Russian sleeping car was typically ornate with over-stuffed seating and the inevitable double curtains on the windows, while my compartment on the Chinese train was very modern and almost spare.

Crossing into Russia on the way to Moscow was an

interesting experience because the gauge of the track changes at the border—from standard gauge which is 4 feet 8.5 inches wide to broad gauge which is five feet wide. As I recall, there were nine cars on our train—eight sleepers and a restaurant car. Trains crossing the border, whether entering or leaving Russia, have to change the wheel assemblies—called "trucks" in the U.S. and "bogies" in Europe—to match the gauge of the track.

At the Russian border, our train was rolled into a long shed four cars at a time. Once carefully positioned with two jacks on each side of each rail car, the rail cars were raised about a foot and the standard gauge bogies were rolled out from underneath.

Next the broad-gauge trucks were rolled into position, two under each car, and the rail cars were then lowered onto its new set of wheels.

There are several reasons given as to why this procedure was considered necessary. One is that when the Russians began building their railways, it was thought that the wider gauge would be an impediment for any invading army attempting to bring massive amounts of men and material into Russia by rail.

Others poo-poo that notion, saying the broader gauge was chosen because it would permit trains to run at higher speeds and with heavier loads. Based on my one-time experience, logic would seem to favor the latter argument since the switch from standard to broad gauge for my train only took about 90 minutes, start to finish.

46

A Sobering Moment

Sometime in the late 1970s, the mayor of Honolulu, Frank Fasi, and five department heads were invited to Pearl Harbor for a briefing about the Navy's state of readiness. Our host was CINCPAC—that's Navy talk for Commander-in-Chief Pacific. At the time, that was Admiral Maurice Weisner.

In the most interesting part of the briefing, we were shown a giant TV screen on which was projected a satellite image of the entire Pacific Ocean. It was covered with dozens of illuminated dots—each representing one ship traveling in the Pacific. For each dot, the Navy knew the name of the vessel, where it was going and how fast it was moving. And no doubt a great deal more than that.

Near the end of the briefing, the officer conducting the session tapped his pointer on a red dot some 200 miles northeast of us. That particular dot, he explained, was a Russian submarine loaded with a dozen or so ballistic missiles, each tipped with a nuclear war head. In fact, in the event of war, the sub's mission was to fire one of its missiles at the very building in which we were sitting at that moment!

There was an uncomfortable silence for several seconds, until one of the city department heads asked what they should do once word came that an attack was imminent... where the people in charge of the critical departments—police, fire, civil defense, and so on—where they should go... a safe place from which to direct their personnel.

The officer hesitated, looking quite uncomfortable. He glanced at Admiral Weisner, who nodded and said, "Continue, Commander."

The officer turned back to the city official and said apologetically, "Well, sir, you do have to bear in mind that this is a very small island."

(Author's note: The Island of Oahu is 44 miles long and 30 miles wide.)

47

Should Politicians Fly First Class?

My blog frequently gets emails from readers, and I enjoy and appreciate their comments. The other day, one of our regulars sent me a brief report on his recent rail journey, and in it he was critical that elements in Congress persist in criticizing Amtrak. That, in turn, led him to state as fact that our elected representatives and other government officials routinely treat themselves to every possible luxury—including first class travel—with our tax dollars footing the bill.

Some of those people do indeed have the idea that they are entitled to special treatment.

Yes, members of Congress are paid well—$174,000 a year for a member of the House—but I do think it's a mitigating factor that most of the members have to maintain two residences: a permanent one in their home district and another in Washington.

And then there's the matter of travel, which is especially burdensome for folks who are elected to Congress from Hawaii.

As a Member of Congress, my friend Neil Abercrombie was extremely conscientious about his job and he understood he had an obligation to spend time in his district office in Honolulu to meet with constituents, deal with their concerns, attend meetings, make speeches and, in general, stay in touch with the people he was representing.

Some of the time, Neil flew with an economy ticket and it's quite true that on many of those occasions, the airline would upgrade him, assuming there was room in First Class. But depending on the time of year and how full the flights were, he did fly First Class and, yes, as far as I know, we taxpayers paid for it.

But the back-and-forth was grueling. Washington-to-Honolulu is a 13-hour trip, and that's under perfect conditions with no delays. Furthermore, heading east, a red-eye is always part of the deal. I must say I really couldn't begrudge Neil the extra comfort of first class. I flew with him once—my little company was handling the media for one of his re-election campaigns—and, while I dozed fitfully, he spent more than half the flight reading official documents and jotting notes.

Neil and I estimated that he made the round trip between Honolulu and Washington from 20 to 25 times a year. And he did that for 20 years. I once figured out that during his time in Congress, Neil Abercrombie had spent almost a year-and-three-months not just "in transit", but literally *in the air!* And much of that time was spent working on the people's business.

48

Ride 'em, Csikós!

On our second visit to Hungary, we added several days to visit the *puszta,* the great plain in the eastern part of the country. It's 800 square kilometers and the largest continuous natural grassland in Europe, all within the *Hortobágyi* National Park.

The Hungarian *puszta* is cattle country and along with sheep and goats, the magnificent gray beasts are the traditional breed still raised in this area. Of course, where there are cattle, there are cowboys. They're called *csikós* in Hungarian (pronounced CHEE-kosh) and I must confess they gave us the most thrilling display of horsemanship I have ever seen, either before or since.

Still wearing the traditional garb, the *csikós* all carry a long bullwhip which they whirl and crack while riding at breakneck speed and driving herds of horses or cattle ahead of them.

Without doubt, the most thrilling performance was one *csikós* driving five horses all galloping at top speed. He was standing on the backs of two horses, holding the reins of all five animals in his left hand, while whirling and cracking his whip in the other.

Before our visit, I had no idea that this part of the Hungarian culture even existed, let alone being a centuries old tradition, originally brought to this part of the world by the Mongols.

Hungary is off the usual tourist itineraries, and Americans who do go there mostly spend just a couple of days in Budapest, but it's a damn shame not to take an extra couple of days to see the *puszta* and the *csikós*... an unforgettable experience.

49

We're Not So Damn Smart

Americans will drive to the airport, park the car for $25 a day, allow two hours to get through security, then catch a 45-minute flight to see relatives for a holiday weekend. Then they'll do it all in reverse to get home. That's how most Americans travel.

Europeans have had transportation issues figured out for a hundred years: They take trains.

Throughout Europe, most inter-city travelers make use of the extensive network of high-speed rail lines, with trains routinely running between most major cities at speeds up to 186 miles per hour.

The fact is, you can get almost anywhere in Europe by train. Big cities and small towns. Several years ago, I spent a couple of days in the town of Azay-le-Rideau in France. As I recall, the population there is about 3500, but they have a railroad station and six trains a day stop there.

Furthermore, European business travelers have figured out

that taking the slower overnight trains can take much of the hassle out of travel and save money, too.

Believe it or not, it's actually possible to do that here in the U.S.

You can hop Amtrak's Capitol Limited in Washington, DC, at 4:05 this afternoon and get to Chicago at 8:45 tomorrow morning in plenty of time for a 10:00 business meeting.

Or leave Washington at 6:50 p.m. on the Silver Meteor and be in Jacksonville, Florida tomorrow morning by 9:10.

Or leave Chicago at 2:00 this afternoon on the California Zephyr and be in Denver for breakfast bright and early tomorrow morning.

I know, I know... it's a bit of a stretch, but it can be done. America could develop a national system of both conventional and high-speed trains that would take cars off the road, make both business and personal travel fast, safe and convenient, and have significant environmental benefits.

But it would mean our politicians would have to summon up a little foresight, a little resolve, and enough humility to acknowledge that there's a helluva lot we could learn from the Europeans. And the likelihood of that is...

50

My Favorite Travel Memory

I suspect that, for most of us who love to travel, there is a place we've been or an incident we've experienced that has some kind of hold on us. For me, it's the memory of a lunch at a small hotel in the medieval town of Domme in southwestern France.

From Gare de Montparnasse in Paris, it was a little over two hours by high-speed train to Bordeaux. A change of trains there and another two-plus hours brought me to Sarlat, where a rental car was reserved.

Leaving Sarlat, the road to Domme crosses a lovely fertile valley, starts a gentle climb, and ends at the massive ancient gate to the town. From there, it's climbing through a labyrinth of stone houses on narrow, one-way streets.

This village of about a thousand people is almost 800 years old. It was built in a defensive location on a mountainous outcropping hundreds of feet above the Dordogne River valley.

And at the end of the road, at the top of the mountain, is the town square and the Hotel L'Esplanade.

It's not luxurious—in fact, a modern luxury hotel would be inappropriate in this setting—but this 15-room property is exactly right: lovingly maintained, beautifully run, and featuring a truly superb restaurant.

But the main feature here is always the extraordinary view of the Dordogne River valley, sweeping probably 120-degrees around the prominence on which the hotel was built and constantly changing with the weather and as the day progresses.

After returning to the hotel, hot and tired from a long morning of sight-seeing, I was led to a choice table on the outdoor patio by the lovely Sophie, the hotel's ever-present owner. She handed me a luncheon menu and I had barely started looking over the choices, when she plucked it from my fingers and said, "I will have an omelette prepared for you!" And she disappeared in the direction of the kitchen.

Ten minutes later, I was absorbed in that view when Sophie returned with what I can only describe as a *perfect* omelette: perfect in presentation, perfect in shape, perfect in texture and taste—light, fluffy, and with a delicate hint of something. In fact, everything about that luncheon was perfect. The lovely day. The incomparable view of the river valley. The ambiance of the hotel patio. The nice glass of white wine. And that perfect omelette.

About the Author

A Hawaii resident for almost 60 years, Jim's career as a professional communicator began in the early 1960s when he was responsible for alumni affairs and public relations for Iolani School. Under his editorship, the school's quarterly magazine was twice named best non-commercial magazine publication in statewide competition.

In 1968, Frank Fasi was elected Mayor of Honolulu and a year later appointed Jim as Director of the Office of Information and Complaint. Jim also served as the mayor's official spokesperson. In the early '70s under Jim's direction, the Mayor's Annual Report took the form of a 60-minute video presentation that was aired on local television stations.

After eight years (and four political campaigns) with Mayor Fasi, Jim accepted a job as General Manager of the Hawaii Islanders, Honolulu's Triple-A professional baseball team, a position he held through the 1979 season.

In 1980, Jim left the Islanders to become vice president and senior account executive for the local advertising firm of Sanders & Printup. Two years later, in partnership with Alan Pollock, Jim formed a new advertising agency which became the largest of Hawaii's mid-sized agencies. Originally known as Loomis & Pollock, the company name was changed to Loomis, Inc. in 1999 when Jim became sole owner of the agency. He retired to Maui a year later.

Jim is a travel author and freelance writer who specializes in rail travel. He has traveled extensively for both business and pleasure, with the train always his preferred choice for transportation. Best estimate: he has logged in excess of 350,000 miles in train travel throughout the world.

He is the author of *Travel Tales*, the popular *All Aboard! The Complete North American Train Travel Guide,* now in its 4th edition, and co-author of *Fascinating Facts About Hawaii.*

Jim served two terms as a member of the Board of Directors of the Railroad Passengers Association and he remains an elected member of the organization's Council of Representatives. A non-partisan, nonprofit organization, RPA advocates for more, better and faster passenger trains in the U.S.

Learn more about Jim, his books and travels at
www.trainsandtravel.com.